The Family in Renaissance Florence

Book Three

Leon Battista Alberti

The Family in Renaissance Florence

Book Three

I Libri Della Famiglia

Translation and Introduction by
Renée Neu Watkins

WAVELAND
PRESS, INC.
Prospect Heights, Illinois

For information about this book, write or call:
    Waveland Press, Inc.
    P.O. Box 400
    Prospect Heights, Illinois 60070
    (847) 634-0081

CONTENTS

INTRODUCTION

The wealthy prodigal lives surrounded by fair-weather friends. "You have seen the water swarming with fish while the bait's afloat; when the bait is gone, all is deserted and empty." The sentiment is attributed to Giannozzo Alberti, a Florentine *pater familias* and chief speaker in Book III. The image is Leon Battista Alberti's own, reflecting the general view of humanity underlying all of his work: the skepticism about people's self-presentation, the withering contempt for mere frivolity, the grief about disloyalty.

The image hints at Alberti's poetic talent and his love of nature, even his love of symmetry. Alberti, after all, was not only a prolific writer of dialogues but also an artist, an architect, and art theorist of enduring fame. He was the very embodiment of the Renaissance man, interested in mathematical principles and in every kind of creative design as well as in social realities—allowing each of his fields of exploration to add some element to the richness of the others. In *Della Famiglia* he expresses moral concerns, hopes and longings for a better social order.

We must recognize that, like many of his less versatile and creative contemporaries, Alberti puts his eloquence into reactionary proposals involving the ever more complete subjugation of women and of the lower orders of mankind. We must also recognize that he deliberately puts those solutions on a completely rational, non-authoritarian and non-religious basis. He intended self-discipline to characterize those who ruled; and honor, moderation, and a penchant for non-violence to make their rule acceptable.

In Alberti's autobiography, (the *Vita*) we are told something of the composition of *Della Famiglia*.[1] The first three books were drafted before he had reached his thirtieth year, he tells us, hence before 1434. He was a secretary in the Papal Curia at the time, and produced the first

[1] Riccardo Fubini and Anna Menci Gallorini, "L'Autobiografia di Leon Battista Alberti," *Rinascimento* 68 (1972), pp. 21–78. For a translation see Renée Neu Watkins, "L. B. Alberti in the Mirror: An Interpretation of the *Vita* with a new translation," *Italian Quarterly* XXX 117 (summer 1989) pp. 5–17.

1

three books in Rome, in ninety days—at break-neck speed. He first circulated them among his own family. His relatives scented the implied criticism of themselves, and their hostility, "decided him to destroy them by fire." He was moved to preserve the work only by the interference of "certain princes."

Thirteen fifteenth-century manuscripts of *Della Famiglia*, one of them a complete copy with the author's revisions in his own hand, are preserved today. The book must have been popular. It was not published, however, until 1734. Even then, only the third book was printed, masquerading under the name of another fifteenth-century Florentine, Agnolo Pandolfini—a mistake that went uncorrected for a hundred years. A printed version with the original interlocutors and the attribution to Alberti saw the light in 1843 in Naples.

In 1845 Anicio Bonucci in Florence published the first three books of *Della Famiglia* in the first volume of his collection of Alberti's *Opere Volgari* (*Works in the Vernacular*). Girolamo Mancini re-edited all four books and published them as a separate text in 1908. This text became a classic used in Italian schools. In 1960 Cecil Grayson made a modern and critical edition. This formed the basis of my translation of all four books, published in 1969 by the University of South Carolina Press. The present volume, in paperback, again isolates Book III, of the four books the most dramatic, far-ranging, and down-to-earth. It is, as R. R. Bolgar put it, "that revealing work where Alberti paints the Florentine merchant class in the fullness of its good sense and sober ostentation."[2]

Della Famiglia III does not, of course, present a single, homogenous bourgeois outlook. As a dialogue it expresses conflicting points of view. It is a monument of attitudes. It enables us to relive social and moral conflicts which troubled early capitalist society. Ponderous and slow of speech, delighting in heavy ironies and elaborate insinuations, Alberti's personages confront much of what it means to be consciously urban—to experience social mobility, to recognize the psychological as well as the practical importance of purchasing various commodities, to wish in vain for stable families and firm public authority amid fluctuating fortunes and alliances.

Alberti's own family—which provides the speakers in the dialogue, *Della Famiglia*, and which is the central subject they discuss—was one

---

[2] R. R. Bolgar, *The Classical Heritage and its Beneficiaries*, Cambridge University Press, 1954, p. 281. (Reprinted by Harper & Row, 1964.)

of the oldest, wealthiest, and most politically prominent merchant clans of Florence. During Alberti's youth, however, due to political battles in the republic, the Alberti were in exile, scattered among various cities where they had commercial contacts. Battista (who later adopted the dignified name of Leo) was born in Genoa in 1404. He was illegitimate, the second son of a liaison between Lorenzo Alberti and a lady of the Genoese patriciate, Bianca di Carolo Fieschi, widow of a Grimaldi.[3] Their father acknowledged his sons and unofficially gave them the Alberti name. When a plague in 1406 took their mother away, Lorenzo removed the boys to Venice. He raised and educated Carlo and Battista, but did not legally legitimize them. While Battista never mentions his illegitimate status, it may well have stimulated the assertive sense of family which he displays in *Della Famiglia*. When he died in 1472 he established, by his will, a residence and stipend in Bologna for members of the Alberti family who might wish to study there.

In May of 1421, Battista's own first year at the University of Bologna, his father, Lorenzo Alberti died. The occasion of that last illness, when many of the family were gathered in his father's house, furnished Battista with the setting of *Della Famiglia*. For Alberti this moment marked the beginning of years of trouble. The loss of his father was soon followed by that of his father's brother and partner, Ricciardo. Battista's cousins, Benedetto and Antonio, took over the branch of the firm formerly managed by Lorenzo and Ricciardo. In the tax registers of Florence for 1430 they state that they had paid less than half the inheritance owed to Battista and Carlo, left in their trust nine years before. It appears from the emphasis on these themes in *Della Famiglia*, that the cousins withheld employment or any other help from the two young men. They claimed to the tax officials that they had spent large sums (almost half the eight thousand gold florins left by Lorenzo) on the boys' education, but Alberti's autobiography and other writings make it clear that they did not. The older cousins also claimed in 1430 to have incurred heavy losses in the trade with Bruges, and ten years later, in fact, the Alberti firm suffered general financial collapse.[4]

---

[3] Carlo Ceschi, "La madre di Leon Battista Alberti," *Bolletino del Arte*, XXXIII (1948), pp. 191–192.

[4] See Roberto Cessi, "Gli Alberti di Padova," *Arch. stor. ital.* ser. 5, XL (1907) pp. 233–284; Girolamo Mancini, *Vita di Leon Battista Alberti*, rev. 2nd ed. Florence, 1911, pp. 51–54; G. A. Holmes, "Florentine Merchants in London, 1343–1450," *Economic History Review*, Second Series XIII (1960), pp. 193–208.

In his autobiography, disguised as an anonymous third person encomium, Battista looks back with indignation on the abject poverty of his student years, when he studied law and, privately, Greek and Latin literature. He became ill from overwork and suffered a temporary loss of memory. Money was not the only issue, for "some of his relatives viciously resented his incipient, nearly established, reputation." They even plotted his death by the hand of a hired assassin. As he sums it up in review: "When he had tried again and again to win over his wicked relatives with many favors and every sort of kindness, he would remark that, actually, he knew full well that another knot won't fix a rotten gangplank."

He kept, aside from his brother, at least one good friend among the Alberti, his cousin Francesco d'Altobianco. Francesco became a partner of Benedetto and Antonio in 1427, but was already being sued by them in Venice in 1436. In 1443 he in turn sued Benedetto's heirs in Florence. Like his more renowned cousin, he wrote for the Florentine poetry contest in the Italian language which Battista helped organize in 1441. They had worked together for some years by then in the papal chancery. To him Battista dedicated Book III of *Della Famiglia*.

The prologue to Book III is optimistic about Italian language and culture, but the prologue to the whole of *Della Famiglia* (both prologues are included in the present edition) expresses a personal and general sense of doom. It dwells on the decline of the family and discusses such problems as declining numbers due to the late marriage of men. (This, by the way, probably implied a fairly large number of illegitimate children.) Laments about the degeneration of the family were not unfamiliar to contemporaries. Preachers complained of fornication, adultery and homosexuality, though not exactly for demographic reasons. Fifty years before *Della Famiglia*, Foligno de' Medici in his book of *Ricordanze* (1373) somewhat prematurely lamented the decline of the Medici.[5] And fifty years later, the London printer William Caxton prefaced his edition of Cato with similar thoughts: "the children . . . encreace and prouffyte not lyke theyr faders and olders."[6] However, among his contemporary humanists, who also wrote on civic life and on education, Alberti was the only one who specifically worried (in writing) about the family as the basic unit of biological and cultural

[5] Quoted by Gene A. Brucker, "The Medici in the Fourteenth Century," *speculum*, XXXII (1957) p. 1.
[6] William Caxton, *The Prologues and Epilogues*, W. J. B. Crotch, ed. London, 1928, p. 77.

continuity. He produced this remarkable analysis, by no means merely a lament, partly in defiance of the obstacles he faced in claiming his own material and social inheritance.

The talk in *Della Famiglia* begins with the dying Lorenzo's concerns about parental responsibility (Book I), then shifts, as other speakers take over, to the bond which biologically underlies all family relationships, sexual love. In Book II Alberti envisages happy marriage as a special case of bonds of close alliance, and attempts to define such bonds. The case for passion is, somewhat ironically, given; the case for reason and calculation mixed with good will wins out. Alberti thus sets the course for Book IV, which, moving to the external relations of the family, is concerned with male friendships. Well calculated, these foster the status of a man and open up opportunities for his descendants.

Book III (here published by itself) deals with the household, which is the basis, if well managed, for the family's prosperity. Under this heading, Alberti reviews, not only the micro-economics of maintaining one's health, house and farm, but the psychology of marriage. How can a husband keep full and unchallenged control of his wife? Likewise, the father's aim in raising children and in managing employees is to gain effective control of outcomes without enmeshing himself in details. He must in all things be foresightful and vigilant, thus resolving problems without needing to have recourse to any kind of violence. Alberti wants the patriarch to assert full control without provoking hostility. His authority is responsible, not arbitrary. Readers are forewarned that all of this discussion of marriage and household reflects the sort of unabashed chauvinism typical of the period's patriarchal point of view. This view is, of course, in strong contrast to modern ideals of fairness and equality. Alberti takes a step toward rationality, but not toward democracy.

Della Famiglia moves at long intervals from one main speaker to another. Each represents not so much a philosophical position as a certain sort of education and a position, defined by age and occupation, in practical life. Alberti thus illustrates the idea that thought does not occur in a vacuum, but grows out of life. In Book I, in the discussion of fatherhood, Adovardo and Lionardo Alberti engage in a kind of debate. Adovardo is forty-five, married, with four children. Lionardo is a bachelor of twenty-nine. The two men interact in a form of duet rather than a duel. The older represents the practical, the younger, the theoretical side of the question. The man of experience dominates. This kind of relationship prevails in all three remaining books. Alberti thus shows great interest (evident also in his works on politics, art and mathematics) in accomplishing a new fusion of knowledge gained from classical books and knowledge gained in the field.

In Book III Lionardo again plays the younger and more bookish interlocutor. He is now, however, humble and almost silent as Giannozzo Alberti's authoritative voice dominates the scene. Gianozzo was a distant relative of Lorenzo, for their great grandfathers were brothers. Sixty-four years old, he speaks of himself as an old man, but one proudly vigorous for his years. He leads an orderly life, with attendance at church and some kind of civic activity included every day, and with plenty of exercise. He is ever engaged in some sort of charitable counseling, and he has had a long experience in business.

This figure reminds us of a remark in the *Vita*, "He [Battista] would see old men of venerable aspect, health and vigor, and never tire of looking at them; this he considered part of his love of the beauties of nature." In Book II Lionardo glorifies man as created by "nature, that is, God," to make use of his capacities, to bear witness to the excellence of his creator by his own excellence. Gianozzo represents the living embodiment of such a fulfillment, at least that is how he sees himself and how the younger men, albeit with a little touch of irony, seem to see and revere him.

Gianozzo's views seemed to Werner Sombart, a social historian and theorist, to represent the very essence and first articulation of "the spirit of capitalism." He matched the teachings of *Della Famiglia III* with those of Benjamin Franklin's *Autobiography*; and it is not possible to deny the many-sided resemblance. There is the same economic vision of moral life, the Stoic self-discipline, the non-Stoic activism, the emphasis on thrift, sobriety, and cleanliness. Both stress the masterful role of the male. It is probably fair to say that Franklin is at once more talkative and repressive about his passions for food and women. It is certain that Franklin is a free and easy self-taught man reaching out to books from an assumed foundation of innate reasonableness. Giannozzo, by contrast, sees himself as relatively uneducated but draws and depends on family tradition, on the oral teachings of earlier venerable elders.

Book III becomes a hymn to *masserizia*—economy, thrift, good management. Giannozzo extends this concept to all things, first applying the notion to those things which "truly belong to us": the body, the soul, and time. These, Giannozzo says, are our only real possessions. Returning to the discussion of practical experience, he detests waste, whether it comes about through prodigality or through irrational stinginess. He demands a total rationalization of the household economy and of its relation to the surrounding world. Giannozzo prescribes a well-balanced private economy including the citizen's private house in the city, his shop, and his villa or farm in the country. Giannozzo considers questions of purchasing, storing and selling food, most of which is to come from one's own country estate. He discusses how to oversee the tenants of such an estate. He emphasizes the principle of buying cheap and selling dear. In the same spirit of economic rationality, he discusses the choice of a young healthy wife and the techniques of training her in good conduct. (Here Alberti applies Xenophon's ancient treatise on the household, *Oeconomicos*, to Florentine habits and conditions.)

Giannozzo is keenly aware of the close relationship between wealth and status—the Renaissance knew as much about self-promotion and public relations as we do today—and he believes that external social factors are determinants of both wealth and status: "friendships" outside the family are necessary for the well-being of the family. He discusses the wisdom of choosing a good respectable neighborhood for your house. Although Giannozzo demands at times Stoic indifference to fortune's cruel tricks, he resolves the basic Renaissance problem of *virtu* and *fortuna*—the problem in modern terms of self against the absurd—by keeping up a continuous dance of adaptation.

All this requires self-discipline, so true thrift includes moderation of the passions. It includes a strong sense of the value of time. Gianozzo also asks the merchant to keep written accounts of everything, and says he admires the merchant with ink-stained fingers. The ideal merchant looks well into the future, is honest, benevolent, generous, but never impetuous or unrestrained. Faced with demands for loans or for standing surety, he makes good use of all sorts of tactics of evasion.

Gianozzo's view of human relations is one that came into its own in the sixteenth-century literature of economic ethics. It indicates, as Benjamin Nelson describes it, "a devaluation of the demands of friendship."[7] Polonius is a later Giannozzo, with his "Neither a lender nor a borrower be . . ." and, as Nelson suggests, his outlook ("to thine own self be true") "can easily be harnessed to the service of a self-regarding capitalist morality."

[7] Benjamin N. Nelson, *The Idea of Usury*, Princeton University Press, Princeton, 1949, p. 155.

The ink-stained fingers of Giannozzo's merchant have led to some speculation about the quality and quantity of literacy among Florentines like Giannozzo. Sombart took them as a sign that the bourgeois of 1420 was still a clumsy fellow with his pen. Armando Sapori, however, an eminent Italian economic historian, asserted that these inky hands belonged to men of considerable fluency, accustomed to write their thoughts as well as their accounts. Alberti stresses that Giannozzo, as a practical man, has no Latin and therefore no classical erudition, by contrast with the young but learned Lionardo. Lionardo flatters Giannozzo for his wisdom whenever the latter expresses feelings of inadequacy before "learned men" or before "you and your books."

Occasionally Giannozzo lets his real pride show: "Thus you young men profit by asking your elders about your problems and hearing their advice. Many things in this world are better understood by experience than by speculation and theory." This seems to be a fundamental conviction of the author, Leon Battista Alberti, as well, and is expressed throughout the interplay of learning and experience in *Della Famiglia*. He favors use of Italian even in writing works of prose that contain plenty of classical wisdom, as this one does in veiled form. He wants the two kinds of knowledge and literacy to mix: he wants popular wisdom to be incorporated in literature and he wants merchants to read more elaborate thinking than was usual in their account books, diaries, memoirs and chronicles.

Alberti's view of Gianozzo is certainly not one of unalloyed admiration. He gives him a strong role as practical counselor, but there is a touch of malice toward both sides in some of the exchanges between Lionardo and Giannozzo, where the former offers effusive flattery and the latter false modesty. When Giannozzo discusses the problem of lending money, or rather of not lending money, he plays the not altogether savory part of sly old fox. There is also a lively discussion of political participation, a delicate question in Cosimo de' Medici's newly tamed Florence. Giannozzo firmly rejects all unnecessary involvement. Public life is full of "pretence, vanity, and lies"; it involves one in cruelty, and leads to unpopularity. "Whether you follow popular thought in its errors or rely on the arrogance of a leader, you are disgraced as though the mistake were your own; even if you labor to serve others, when you please one, you displease a hundred." And more incisively, "A man wants to live for himself, not for the community." Lionardo, the learned young man, distinguishes between mere powerlust and true public spiritedness. "Like you," he answers Giannozzo, "I would say that a good citizen loves tranquillity, but not so much his own tranquillity as that of other good men, rejoices in his private leisure, but does not care less about that of his fellow citizens than about his own. He desires the unity, calm, peace, and tranquillity of his own house, but much more those of the country and of the republic."

There is another interesting argument, toward the end of *Della Famiglia III*, this time between Giannozzo and Adovardo. The latter is kind, urbane, temperate, and eager to impart the fruit of both reading and experience. In age he represents a generation between Giannozzo and Battista. Adovardo seems to represent the author most closely in that he corrects the weaknesses of the others and exalts an arduous and subtle magnanimity. His argument with Giannozzo is about money.

Giannozzo builds a picture of economics in which commodities are (as Ricardo and Marx were to expound) the result of labor applied to fortune's gifts. The merchant's markup is the payment of his labor. Some commodities are primarily gifts of fortune, especially the direct fruits of the soil; others are primarily services. All bring profit if and only if properly managed. Giannozzo makes money another commodity, essentially one that carries the service of exchange. According to him, in direct contradiction to Thomas Aquinas, it breeds profit as naturally as cows produce calves. Good management is essential in both cases.

For Giannozzo, as Adovardo remarks with amazement, money has no special role. It is a commodity like any other. To Adovardo it is something special, the key to all other commodities. Well managed, unlike any other gift of fortune or product of labor, it is practically contingency-proof. In a world of perishables, only money is an abstract form of wealth which keeps profit coming. This, in fact, is the key to capitalistic expansion and conquest. Adovardo, that is, suggests the philosophy of investment bankers, as distinct from Giannozzo, who represents the general merchant. Lionardo, youngest of them all, had already explained in Book II that large profits come only from large investments in large-scale commerce. All three speakers admire hard work, seeing labor—mainly the labor of management—as the source of value. Adovardo alone really explains what it means to have not fixed, but fluid wealth.

On the whole, in *Della Famiglia III* Alberti presents an idealized image of the merchant class that dominates Florence. It consists of powerful urban men dealing justly and prudently with others of their class, while controlling and protecting their "natural" subjects: women, children, servants, employees and tenants. All inferior classes present problems of insubordination, cheating, and the creation of disorder. Socially above the powerful urban men and dangerously powerful through brute force are the members of the landed and titled aristocracy, often the rulers and controllers of armies. The merchants must prevent these as best they can from carrying out robbery and pillage. The merchants are more concerned than traditional rulers of land with maintaining a well-ordered and peaceful society.

Through such characters as Giannozzo and Adovardo, Alberti voices some precepts for dealing with human beings. Like Machiavelli almost a century later, Alberti combines literary authorities and practical experience to teach what works, what leads to success. At least once, through Giannozzo, he dismisses a high philosophical ideal, that of friendship, simply because such friendships are rare or nonexistent. The purpose and method affect the substance of the dialogue. Like Machiavelli, Alberti implies that ultimately the individual owes no one anything: one is born for one's own happiness. This is the implicit message, even though the explicit wisdom represents men who govern others in a humane way.

The father of the family governs it well because he wants the glory of his name to shine and to last. He makes sure that wife and children and servants perform their functions well, because he makes it clear that their own advantage depends on following his guidance. He not only has the power to withdraw his support if they do not obey, but he has the wisdom to see that everyone does what he or she is naturally best at doing. Thus he reconciles their need for glory with his own. Enlightened self-interest, especially the desire for honor, is the foundation for social harmony. For one's own happiness, a man or woman will work, and even work unselfishly. Machiavelli did not keep this pleasant and precarious reconciliation of the moral and the expedient.

For Alberti virtue (*virtu*) is linked to aesthetic goals such as balance and harmony, as well as to ethical interaction within a peaceful and efficient hierarchical system. Alberti certainly means his *virtu* to correspond to the Greek *arete* and the Latin *virtus*, but he chooses to give it a looser, more pragmatic and concrete significance than these words carry in Plato and Cicero. Plato's sharp definitions lead to the reader's giving up commonplace ideas of good for a more rigorous theory of means and ends. In conscious contradiction to ancient philosophers, *Della Famiglia* suggests that intelligent men of the world, if not people in general, admire and even reward real virtue. Virtue here embodies a curious combination of the shrewdness that brings success in worldly matters and the qualities of soul that, without normally sacrificing such success, go beyond it. The basis of the description of virtue here is the familiar reality of Florentine psychological experience: the bourgeois sense of honor.

The essential convictions running through *Della Famiglia* brought Alberti into the Florentine world. He boasts in the *Vita* that his fellow Florentines borrowed felicitous phrases from *Della Famiglia* for their speeches in the Signoria, or ruling council, of Florence—a real tribute to an author just returned from life-long exile. Alberti had seen deeply and convincingly into their moral world.

To the agonistic society built around commercial capitalism, he offers three major consolations for the inevitable damage to trust and to stability done by fierce competition, the inevitable sense of living in a dog-eat-dog world that particularly appears in Giannozzo's speeches. First, he makes us believe that competition itself, since it teaches *masserizia* (or good management) is generally for the betterment of all participants, win or lose. Second, we learn that the family, the fundamental social unit, may seem to be falling apart but it will not be destroyed in the universal struggle. On the contrary, by functioning effectively, it assures its survival and that of its members. Third, whether success be fast or slow in coming, the freedom and dignity, the self-convinced autonomy of the individual, thrives as long as he practices *virtu*, which is the basis of his self-respect. Therefore, the bourgeois ethic as Alberti formulates it, postulates a rather favorable view of society's discretion in rewarding the good, and of human character in maintaining each man's moral independence. All that idealization of life in the patriciate makes the book a more perfect gift to them. Alberti himself never married or ran a business, nor did he reside for long in the Florence to which he felt that he belonged. He was by necessity a courtier and by choice an artist, active in various republics and principalities. From his own way of living it seems, as well as from the tradition of classical humanism, he drew values that enhance the message of his semi-fictional Gianozzo, Lionardo and Adovardo.

Under the bourgeois and mercantile surface, *Della Famiglia III* expresses other truths as well. Harmony and dissonance of ideas create a rough and interesting music. Gianozzo arguing shrewdly and gently with his younger cousins, who are children of exile and of advanced education, foreshadows the worldly and smug courtier Polonius. His younger relatives, while not as self-disclosing as Hamlet, manifest some of that prince's insecurity. Perhaps after all, besides the merchant ethic that these personages claim to define, we should notice the stance of an old man of established position facing young men who are not so much cleverer capitalists as younger strivers. They are struggling up the ladder of ambition in the Medici-run state or in other hierarchies. There are many ways of reading *Della Famiglia III* and of sharing with the interlocutors their evident sadness, pride, irritation, and sense of triumph over the odds.

GENERAL PROLOGUE

call to mind what ancient records and the recollection of our elders, as well as our own experiences, can teach us. Many families in Italy and elsewhere have been seen first at the height of fortune and honor, then lying prostrate, reduced and exhausted. Often I have marveled and sorrowed that fortune's cruelty and ill will seemed to have such power over men. Fortune's fickleness and imprudence actually seemed able to seize families rich in heroes, abounding in all that is precious, dear, and most desired by mortal men, endowed with honor, fame, high praise, authority, and public favor, and to cast them down into poverty, desolation, and misery. They were reduced from a great number of ancestors to a very few descendants, from unmeasured riches to strait necessity, and hurled from the brightest splendor of glory. They were drowned in calamity, plunged into obscure, oblivious, tempestuous adversity. How many families do we see today in decadence and ruin! It would not be possible to enumerate and describe all the most noble families among the ancients, like the Fabii, Decii, Drusii, Gracchi, and Marcelli and others. They stood in our land for the public good, for the maintenance of liberty, and for the conservation of authority and dignity in peace and in war. They were modest, wise, and fortunate families, feared by their enemies, but loved and revered by their friends. Of all these families not only the magnificence and greatness but the very men, not only the men but the very names are shrunk away and gone. Their memory, almost every trace of them, is wiped out and obliterated.

For these reasons I have always thought the question worth asking whether fortune really has such power over human affairs. Is the supreme license hers in fact, by her inconstancy and instability, to plunge the greatest and most admirable families into ruin? I think about this matter objectively, with a mind detached and free of passion, and consider, O, young Albertis, our own Alberti family. I consider the great calamities to which it has now for so long opposed a noble fortitude, and integrity of

heart and intellect. Thus have our Albertis been able to throw off or endure with constancy bitter misfortunes and furious blows from a cruel
fate. I see clearly then that fortune has too often been unjustly blamed. I
observe that many who have fallen on evil days by their own folly have
accused fortune. They complain of being buffeted by her stormy seas
when they themselves, most foolishly, threw themselves into the flood.

If anyone undertakes to investigate the nature of those things which
exalt and increase the family, and to see how it is maintained at a high
level of honor and happiness, he soon discovers that men are most
inclined to view themselves as cause of their own good or poor estate.
They will never attribute so much influence to anything as to deny, in the
end, that praises, greatness, and fame are won more by character than by
fortune. If we think about the republics and principalities of the past, we
shall find that to acquire and augment power and glory, to preserve and
keep them once won, fortune was never more important for any state
than good and pious traditions of conduct. Who would deny it? Just laws,
virtuous princes, wise counsels, strong and constant actions—these are
effective. Love of country, fidelity, diligence, highly disciplined and
honorable behavior in the citizens—these have always been able, even
without the help of fortune, to earn and kindle fame. With fortune's
help, they have enabled countries vastly to extend their domain, to
expand with increased glory, mightily to commend themselves to poster-
ity, to immortality.

Fortune favored the Macedonians and made them prosper as long as
they maintained the use of arms together with the love of virtue and the
desire for glory. True it is that after the death of Alexander the Great, as
soon as the Macedonian kings began to pursue only their private good
and to care not for the public empire but for their own kingdoms, discord
arose and burning flames of hate were kindled among them. Their spirits
were consumed with greed and fury. They longed to do harm and to take
vengeance. Then those same arms and triumphant hands which had
seized and subjected the liberty and the strength of innumerable peoples,
which had built so great an empire, by which the name and fame of
Macedonia had become world famous, these same undefeated arms,
serving the private appetites of a few hereditary tyrants, were the ones to
tear up and scatter every law, every justice and excellence they had
instituted. They cut through every tendon of their once feared strength.
Thus the Macedonians destroyed, not by fortune but by folly, the happiness they had attained. Soon they found themselves without empire and

without glory. Greece kept her victory, glory, and empire just as long as she was zealous and vigorous in ruling, eager to govern and discipline the minds of her citizens, not just to crown herself with delights and lord it over others with pompous ceremonies.

Is not our Italian situation clearly of the same kind? For a long time we observed our best and most hallowed traditions. We labored to make ourselves the equals of our ancestors and even to outshine the glory of their past achievements. Our citizens thought that they owed to their country all labor, diligence, and art, that all they had should serve the public welfare and provide reward and sustenance for the whole community. Our possessions, blood, and life were willingly poured out to maintain the authority, majesty, and glory of the Latin name. Was there any people anywhere, even the most savage nation of barbarians, which did not fear and obey our edicts and laws? This marvellous empire without limits, this lordship over all peoples acquired by our Latin forces, obtained by our diligent efforts, increased by our Latin armies, can it be said to have been granted us as a gift of fortune?

Shall we admit that what our character won for us we owe to fortune? Shall we ascribe to fortune the prudence and moderation of Fabius, whose delaying and passive tactics saved our almost captured Latin liberty? What of the justice of Tarquin, who, to maintain military discipline, refused a pardon to his son? What of the purity of a man who, content with a farmer's life, preferred honesty to any amount of gold? What of the stern justice of Fabritius, the temperance of Cato, the fortitude of Horatio Cocles, the sufferings of Mutius, the faith and piety of Regulus, the patriotism of Curtius? What of the other remarkable, excellent, and incredible virtues of soul that were praised and honored among the ancients? Shall we ascribe to fortune sacred qualities which worked no less than iron and violence to let our noble Italian ancestors subdue the peoples of every barbarous region? With these did they subjugate the proud and stubborn barbarian enemies of Latin liberty, glory, and name.

Shall we view fortune, then, as the teacher of morals, the moderator of conduct, and the guardian of our most sacred traditions? Shall we consider subject to fortune's fickle and arbitrary will these standards which men, with mature wisdom and with hard and painful efforts, set up for themselves? How can we say that fortune, with her equivocal ways and her inconstancy, can ruin and destroy the very works which we most want to subordinate to our own watchfulness and reason, and not to another's whim? How shall we admit that what we fervently and laboriously strive to maintain belongs to fortune rather than to us? It is not in fortune's power, it is not as easy as some foolish people believe, to conquer one who really does not want to be conquered. Fortune has in her hand only the man who submits to her.

At Cannae, Trebbia, Trasimenus, in the Gauls, in Spain, and elsewhere, fortune in various ways rose up to fight against the Latin armies with no less cruelty and inhumanity than our most savage enemies. She exerted all her might to crush us and stamp out our empire, our glory, and all Italy. Nonetheless the empire grew from day to day by a wondrous series of rapid and numerous triumphs. Who can count exactly how often, then and later, fortune herself was wicked and hostile? She certainly raised up the envy of peoples, of kings, and of nations against us and provoked spite and enmity toward us in all the world. Her furious and bestial attacks could never daunt the courage of the good Roman patrician senators. They fought down and transcended every danger to become the lords and masters of all proud peoples. They divided the world into provinces. They set the bounds of the Latin empire outside the very limits and borders of the earth.

Our Latin forefathers, then, were able to oppose and to sustain every attack of fortune. Their noble spirits never gave up the will, and with the will the power, and with the power the ability to achieve expansion and glorious success. Though the course of their great triumphs was often interrupted by envious fortune, their history was never lacking in high heroism. As long as they considered good works and the strict moral traditions of their fatherland the ornament and the enduring strength of their empire, fortune, too, always proved favorable in the end. They continued to enjoy both imperial glory and good fortune as long as they possessed lofty and pious spirits, grave and mature counsel, perfect faith and loyalty toward the fatherland—as long as concern for the public good outweighed with them the pursuit of private ends, as long as the will of the state overruled the individual's desires.

As soon as lust for personal power and individual pleasures, as soon as unjust desires counted for more in Italy than good laws and the hallowed habits of restraint, the Latin empire grew weak and bloodless. It lost its grace and splendor and all its original strength. Latin glory, which once had shed its light beyond the very bounds of Ocean and lighted all the world, became cloudy and obscure. You, O noble Italy, were the crown and citadel of all the world while you were united, agreed, harmoniously determined on the preservation of your high virtues and on the achievement of renown and increase of glory. You used all your zeal and skill to conquer proud peoples and to govern nations with humanity and justice once you had subjected them. You bore every adversity with a proud and upright spirit. You thought it more praiseworthy to suffer and win in some hard and arduous enterprise than to disdain such painful labors. You showed your enemies your strength, your friends your loyalty, and your subjects your mercy. Thus you overcame fortune and rose above all mortal men. You proclaimed sacred laws and appointed governors in all the nations of the earth. To the very borders of India you were able to erect shining monuments to your immeasurable, divine, and well-earned glory. For your excellent qualities, for your magnificent, courageous, and mighty spirit, were you like gods revered and loved and feared.

After this you suddenly began to decline from your former majesty. Your Latin altars, temples, and theaters were long the scene of games and banquets and of rejoicing, long laden to groaning with the tribute of enemies, the votive offerings of victors, the triumphant laurels. Suddenly all these began to witness sorrow and misery, to be washed with tears and to resound with mourning and lamenting. The barbarian nations, distant slave peoples which formerly put aside pride and anger to tremble when they heard your venerated name, O Italy, now they were puffed up with boldness. They burst into your very heart, most sacred Italy, to burn the nest, the ancient seat of the empire of empires.

Other nations have usurped our empire by our negligence and laziness, or we have shed and abandoned our once deserved glory. Now who would dare hope ever to recover our lost imperial scepter, or expect to see again the purple and the diadem restored to their sacred and most happy home here in Italy. To our reproach they have here been long and sorely missed. Who could fail to conclude that the great glory of the Latin name was removed from its natural setting through no other fault than our own? What multitude of people could have opposed the power that all the world obeyed?

We know, then, that fortune is weak and powerless when it comes to taking away the least part of our character. Nobility of soul, we cannot but recognize, is itself sufficient to ascend and to possess the highest peaks: glorious praise, eternal fame, immortal glory. It seems undeniable that nothing is easier to acquire than this nobility, if only you seek it and value it. Only he who does not want it is without virtue. Character, discipline, and manly labor are available to men as much as they want. Good counsel, wisdom, strong and constant and persevering spirits, reason, order, method, good arts and skills, equity, justice, diligence, and zeal permeate and animate the greatest empire and overcome the might of deceitful fortune to achieve the highest degree, to take the last fortresses of glory. O young Albertis, how can any of you think to convince me, by appealing to the frequently observed fickleness and brittleness of imper- manent things, that the noble character, which cannot be denied to men as long as they use judgment and will to seize and to hold that which is by nature a true possession of men, can be easily taken away from zealous and vigilant possessors, from proud and strong defenders? We shall always believe that in political affairs and in human life generally reason is more powerful than fortune, planning more important than any chance event. I believe it is your own opinion as well, for you are all prudent and wise. Nor have I ever thought a man wise or prudent who put his faith in chance situations rather than in character. Men must see that industry, skill, persevering labors, wise counsel, honest activity, just demands and reasonable expectations do maintain and defend both republics and prin- cipalities. With these any empire can rise to glory, while without them it inevitably remains empty of majesty and honor. When one realizes that laziness, inertia, lust, deceit, cupidity, iniquity, the raw appetites and unrestrained passions of men are what infects, subverts, and undermines every solid and well founded human endeavor, one must also, I think, see that these truths apply as much to families as they do to kingdoms. One is forced to admit that families rarely fall into decrepitude through any other cause than their own lack of wisdom and energy.

This much I know, that fortune's cruel floods quickly submerge and destroy the family that throws itself upon those waves either by abandon- ing restraint and moderation in prosperity or by lacking a firm posture and a prudent self-control in the face of hostile storms. I also have no doubt at all that by good management, careful and diligent rule by the father, good habits, and the utmost integrity of conduct, culture, courtesy, and responsibility, the family can become great and fortunate. I have undertaken, therefore, to investigate with all seriousness and diligence what might be the wisdom, applicable to the conduct and education of fathers and of the whole family, by which a family may rise at last to supreme happiness. Thanks to such wisdom it should under no circum- stances have to yield to cruel and merciless fortune.

All the time I have been able to take from my other duties, I have been happy to spend going through the ancient authors to find whatever right and relevant thoughts they have left us to further the welfare, honor, and greatness of our families. Since I did find many excellent lessons there, I took it upon myself to compile and order them in such a way that you might come to know them with little trouble. Having come to know them, you might take them to heart. I think, too, that when you have reviewed with me the sayings and authority of the great writers of antiquity and considered the excellent customs of our own Alberti ancestors, you will conclude, as I have done, that your fortune, along with your character, depends on you. You will also be pleased, as you read me, to discover what were the noble ancient ways and beliefs of our Alberti house. When you see that the counsels and remembered customs of the older members of the family are all excellent and highly applicable, you will admire and follow them yourselves. You will learn how the family may multiply to live happily and well. You will see what practices bring the family favor, popularity, and friends. It will be clear by what kind of conduct the family gains a wide reputation, fame, and glory. You will see how the family name may achieve everlasting glory and immortality.

Let no one suppose, however, that I have the impudence to consider myself your teacher in matters of such importance, as if your own reason and discretion did not fully instruct you. I have always realized that everyone of you far surpasses me in intelligence and in learning and in knowledge of great and high matters. I admit that to you there is little I could teach, and that there is less I could remember that you do not know and remember better than I. Still it may not be a vain ambition which has prompted me to give many a day to this laborious endeavor. I hope to be of some use at least to the younger members of the family who will be coming along. In truth I should like my efforts to please you no little. I should hope that even if this work were not to be as useful to the Alberti family as it will be, it would be my great honor to be frequently read by you. This would be my greatest possible reward. It would especially satisfy me if you understand what I am so eager to convey, that all my desire and expectation is aimed at nothing but making myself as well liked by you as I can. Indeed I hope to be much better liked and accepted by you.

I have convinced myself that Battista cannot but please you. As far as possible I have applied my imagination and energy to make myself better from day to day, more useful to you, and more dear to your hearts. This will also give me incentive to labor on with still greater vigor and zeal. I shall keep still more vigils, exercise still more painstaking care, in order one day to delight your judgment and fulfill your hopes with some more perfect, more polished work. This is what I shall do, indeed, if I see that you appreciate, as I think you ought to appreciate, the lessons given us by our Alberti ancestors. These you will find most noble and worthy of memory. I shall be encouraged if you esteem me also for being most eager to keep alive the true honor and well-founded glory of our Alberti family. It has always merited appreciation and praise, and to its name I have always devoted all my efforts, my labors, my thoughts, my intellect and will. Never, as long as there is art or power in me, will I spare myself fatigue or exertion or any strenuous effort that may prove good or useful to the Alberti family. I shall labor the more happily, eagerly, and industriously if only I see them glad to receive my work. So I ask you young Albertis to join me in what I know you are doing already: seek the well-being, increase the honor, magnify the fame of our house. Listen, also, to what our Alberti ancestors thought that learned, educated, cultivated persons owed to the family. See what they remind us should be done. Read me and take me to your hearts.

Prologue to Book III
to Francesco d'Altobianco Alberti

Francesco, your uncle, Messer Antonio Alberti, a most learned man, used often to walk in those lovely gardens of yours with his learned friends and discuss, as our father, Lorenzo Alberti, told us, which was the greater loss, the fall of our ancient, most extensive empire, or the dying out of our ancient, most beautiful Latin tongue. Our father himself never doubted but that the loss to our Italian people of the general respect and obedience once given us as a natural tribute to our excellence was a far lighter misfortune than the fact of finding ourselves shorn of a flourishing language in which so many great writers had recorded their lofty knowledge of the good and blessed way to live. In our ancient empire there certainly was some wondrous grace and majesty, for it gave sound justice and perfect equity to all peoples; yet a prince probably derived, from the eminence of that position which he held by fortune's favor, no more power and authority than from his knowledge of the Latin language and familiarity with Latin letters. We might add that perhaps it was no great wonder if the nations, with their natural love of liberty, in time withdrew their submission to us and stubbornly fought against and overthrew our dictates and our laws. But by whose fault but our own could anyone explain this other calamity, the loss of something which no one took from us and no one stole? It even seems to me that our imperial splendor was not wholly extinguished until the light and the far-reaching influence of Latin and of Latin letters faded away. Strange indeed that a thing preserved by use came to be corrupted and diminished while still, in those days, certainly current among all men.

It may perhaps be thought a consequence of the other catastrophes that then befell us. Italy was repeatedly occupied and subjected to various nations: the Gauls, the Goths, the Vandals, the Lombards, and other like harsh and barbarous peoples. As necessity or the wish to communicate prompted them, therefore, people learned one foreign language or another, partly just to be understood and partly to please in their manner of speaking persons whom they had to obey. The foreigners, meanwhile, being newly arrived, also adapted their ways to ours, with considerable admixture, I believe, of barbarisms and corruptions. This mixing, then, made our originally refined and polished language grow from day to day more rustic and degenerate.

I do not think we should accept the idea of some people, however, who find this loss so astonishing that they claim there was in Italy, even in those times and earlier, only the language that we employ today. They cannot believe that the women in those days knew things which are obscure and difficult even for the most learned scholars today. They therefore conclude that the language in which men of education wrote was only an academic and artificial invention, understood but not truly used by many people. Were this the place to debate the question, I would ask these people who among the ancients ever wrote, not of scholarly and learned matters but of everyday, domestic things to his wife or children or servants in any language but Latin? Who, I would also ask, ever used in private or public communication any but this form of speech in which, because it was common to all, they in fact wrote all they had to say, whether to the general public or to friends. I would ask them, further, whether they think foreigners today find our present language less difficult to use with precision and clarity than we the ancient tongue? Don't we see with what difficulty our slaves learn to employ our own idioms comprehensibly simply because, in their unfamiliarity with our variations of case and tense, they do not know how to make words agree as required? How many women in those days were highly praised for their good Latin; indeed, the speech of almost all women was praised above that of men for being less contaminated by contact with foreigners! How many orators there were, too, who were entirely unversed in anything academic and totally illiterate! Why, moreover, would the ancient writers, when they were taking such pains to be of use to their fellow citizens, have written in a language known only to a few? This hardly seems to be the place, however, to discuss this subject at length; perhaps we may argue it more fully elsewhere. Yet no true scholar will deny the only sound hypothesis, I think, namely that all the ancient writers, when they wrote as they did, wished to be understood by all their contemporaries.

If that is how it was, my learned friend Francesco, and you agree with me, what need have we to fear the criticism of a few ignorant readers? Who, on the other hand, will dare to say that I should not have written in a language which permits the ignorant to read me? The wise, indeed, are more likely to praise my zeal if, by writing so that all could understand, I have made an effort rather to educate many than to please a few, for you know how few these days are the educated. How pleased I would be, indeed, if my vociferous critics were capable of earning praise as well as of condemning others. I fully admit that the ancient Latin language was rich and beautiful, but I see no reason why our present-day Tuscan is so contemptible that anything written in it, however excellent, should fail to satisfy us. I think it will do for me if I can say approximately what I want to say and speak in a manner that may be understood. These critics' own knowledge of the ancient tongue, meanwhile, extends only to keeping silent in it, and of the modern to maligning those who do not keep silent. Here is my view: if someone else be more learned than I, or be what many would like to be thought to be, he will find our common tongue no less beautiful than the one they so much prefer and wish to force on everyone. I cannot approve of the contempt so many people show for what they themselves speak, while they praise what they neither understand nor cultivate by reading. It is not honorable to demand of others what you refuse to do yourself. As to the great authority among all nations which my critics attribute to the ancient language, this authority exists simply because many learned men have written in it. Our own tongue will have no less power as soon as learned men decide to refine and polish it by zealous and arduous labors.

I do not try to hide from the comprehension and, with it, the criticism of all our fellow citizens. Let my adversaries either quell their envious spirit or take more valuable matter and prove their own eloquence in it. Anyone should prefer to apply his energies to something better than maligning those who do not stagnate in idleness. I do not hope to be praised for more than my good will in attempting, as far as my intelligence, industry, and zeal permit, to make some useful contribution to our Alberti family. I think it is more valuable to work as I do, by writing, than by silence to escape the criticism of those who cry me down.

Therefore, Francesco, as you know, I have already written two books, in the first of which you learned how, in the well-conducted family, elders exercise care and discretion in the training of the young, and the young, in turn, behave as they are obliged and duty-bound to do toward their elders. There you saw what diligence is required of fathers and mothers in the bringing up of their offspring to good behavior and high character. My second book set forth what are the chief considerations in marrying, and discussed the proper occupations for young men. So far, then, we have made the family large and set it on the road to success; now, since good management is reputed to be extremely important if wealth is to be well enjoyed, here is this third book. Here you will find a description of a proper *pater familias*. I think you will not find it tedious. You will notice the bare simplicity of the style, and in this you will recognize that I have done my best to imitate the charming and delightful Greek writer Xenophon. You, Francesco, since you have always held me dear and liked my works, will read this good *pater familias* and learn from him how to rule and preserve your own person, first of all, and then whatever you possess.

You will understand, of course, that I am not attempting by the gift of this book—a pledge and symbol of our friendship—to repay all that your goodness has been to me. As you can imagine, I shall consider myself more than ever in your debt if you will take the trouble to read and correct this work. With your help there will be so much the less for our adversaries to use against us. Read me, my dear Francesco, and love me as ever.

BOOK THREE

Liber Tertius Familie: Economicus

ionardo had already answered our questions on a number of points where Carlo and I, on thinking over the discussion of the previous evening as reported above, had found ourselves doubtful or puzzled as to what he had said. He had begun to praise warmly the diligence of our efforts, for Carlo and I had made notes during the night of the discussion we had heard. Now Giannozzo Alberti arrived on the scene. Here was a man whose humane and noble conduct made everyone call him a good man, as in truth he was. He came to see Ricciardo. He greeted us and asked how Lorenzo was feeling and how he had responded to the consolation of seeing his brother. Lionardo gave him reverent welcome, and said,

I would have been happy, Giannozzo, had you been with us last night, when Ricciardo arrived.

Giannozzo: I, too, would have been glad to be here, but I did not know of it in time.

Lionardo: Your heart, I assure you, would have been touched. Lorenzo's condition was serious indeed, to tell the truth, and he was very weak, Giannozzo. This illness of his grows heaviest toward evening and burdens him then more gravely than in the daytime. Lorenzo heard and recognized his brother's voice, and he tried, in the manner of a most weary man, to raise himself up. He lifted both his eyes, and one hand he raised enough to uncover the whole arm. He held it up for a moment and let it fall, sighed, turned his gaze toward his brother, looked upon him with great fervor, and weak as he was, did what he could to show his brother an honorable welcome. He gave him his hand; Ricciardo drew closer, and they embraced and held each other close for quite some time. Each

25

seemed to want to speak to the other and to say various things, but they could not say anything. They wept.

Giannozzo: Ah, for pity's sake.

Lionardo: Then they let each other go. Ricciardo did all he could to hide his weeping. Lorenzo, after a little while, spoke to him, and these were his first words, "My brother, Battista here and Carlo will be your children from now on." No one among us could restrain his tears any longer.

Giannozzo: The pity of it. And Ricciardo?

Lionardo: You can imagine.

Giannozzo: Cruel fortune. But how is Ricciardo now?

Lionardo: Fine, as far as I saw.

Giannozzo: I came to see him.

Lionardo: I think at this moment he is resting.

Giannozzo: How unlike the old Ricciardo to be idly sleeping. I think I never knew a man livelier or more devoted to work than Ricciardo.

Lionardo: Don't be surprised, Giannozzo, if Ricciardo lies in bed late today. He went to bed very late last night, exhausted by travel and his mind, too, probably much burdened with many troubled thoughts.

Giannozzo: It's true we old fellows find the slightest exertion a painful strain. I feel it myself even now. This morning at dawn I went up to the Palazzo to plead for the honor and property of a friend. It was not yet time for the business I wanted to do, so I came down here quickly. If, during this interlude, I might greet Ricciardo, I would go back to the temple to see the sacrifice and worship God, then return to do what my friend needs to have done. Yet I am already exhausted, I am weary through and through. The truth is that the winter season treats us very differently from the trees, for winter lightens the trees, unclothing and stripping them of leaves, but to us old men winter brings heavy burdens and clothes us in shadow and in pain. Thus it is, my children, that the longer one lives, the more one weeps in this world. That friend of mine, he, too, feels the weight of the years and of poverty, and if I did not undertake to carry a part of his burden, God knows in what dire state he would be.

Lionardo: I have heard our kinsmen, and others as well, call you a good man, Giannozzo. Now I see they have good reasons, and that you particularly merit the name for your unwearying interest in helping your friends, supporting the needy, coming to the aid of those in trouble. But sit, Giannozzo. You are tired, and it befits your age to be seated. Sit down.

Giannozzo: Yes, so I shall. But you should understand, Lionardo, it is only in the last few years that I have come to this. I just can't do as much as I used to.

Lionardo: And how many things didn't you do in your youth which you would no longer want to do now? Other things give you pleasure now, perhaps, which did not appeal to you then.

Giannozzo: Many, my dear Lionardo. I vividly remember how in my youth, in those days when our country was in a prosperous state, jousting or public games were frequent. There always used to be sharp disagreements between my elders and myself because I wanted, above all things, to go along with the others into the midst of it all and prove my worth. The men from our house always came home with high praises and honor. I enjoyed their triumph myself, it is true, yet I also grieved because I was not among those whose noble exertions won the honors. Oh, the Alberti family more than any other great family of florence sent young men into the field. I used to watch them, joyful, spirited, full of strength as they performed feats of arms. The whole people seemed to care only for the Alberti men; they did not know how to applaud a man who was not an Alberti; everyone felt that if anyone else was praised, anyone who was not a member of our clan, it was honor stolen from us. You can imagine how I delighted in the great acclaim thus enjoyed, and justly, by our men. Imagine, on the other hand, Lionardo, how a youth with a lively and manly spirit such as I then possessed would suffer at being prevented from taking his own place among his kinsmen as he longed to do, and making everyone praise and admire him. Thus did I suffer.

I hated everyone who kept me away from the joust, and every word my elders spoke seemed a stone smiting my ears, Lionardo. I could not listen to what they said when they all warned me that jousting was dangerous, useless, expensive, more apt to produce envy than love, more likely to bring a man shame than fame, that too many accidents happened, that quarrels arose there, and that they held me more dear than I thought or, indeed, deserved. And I—silent, sullen. Then they would tell me many a tale of men who came out of those maneuvers dead or broken, useless for the rest of their lives. You would laugh if I told you how many devices I hit on to gain their permission, for I still would not have done this, or anything else, without the permission of my elders. I would get kinsmen, friends, and friends of friends to intercede with them for me. I said that I had promised, and produced persons who confirmed my having sworn it to my companions. Nothing helped. Thus there were times when I did not love them as I usually did. I well knew that they did all this because I was all too dear to them, and because they, in their love, feared lest some disaster befall either my person or my honor, as often happens to a strong and courageous boy. Yet did they seem hateful to me when they opposed me and stood firm against my too obstinate, though manly will. I was angrier still whenever I thought they acted as they did from motives of economy, for they were, as you know, excellent and careful managers, as I, myself, have since learned to become. In those days I was young, I spent and gave away my money.

Lionardo: And now?

Giannozzo: Now, my dear Lionardo, I have become wise. I know that it is madness to throw away what you possess. The man who has never experienced the sorrow and frustration of going to ask others for help in his need has no idea of the usefulness of money. If a man has no experience to tell him how painfully money is acquired, moreover, he spends it with ease. If a man spends without measure, he is usually quickly impoverished. And if a man lives in poverty, my children, he will suffer want and many deprivations, such is this world, and perhaps he would be better off dying than living in need and misery. Therefore, dear Lionardo, believe me, as one who knows by experience and could not have more certain knowledge, the proverb of our peasants is most true: "He who finds no money in his own purse will find still less in another's." It is most desirable my dear children to be thrifty. One should guard against too great spending as if it were a mortal foe.

Lionardo: Yet I think, Giannozzo, that with all your desire to avoid expense, you would still wish neither to be nor to appear avaricious.

Giannozzo: God forbid. Let our worst enemies be avaricious. There is nothing like avarice to destroy a man's reputation and public standing. What virtue is so bright and noble but that, under the cloak of avarice, it is wholly obscured and passes unrecognized. A hateful anxiety perpetually troubles the spirit of a man who is too tightfisted and avaricious. Whether he be worriedly gathering or reluctantly spending his wealth, he has always a great gnawing and heavy burden. He lives in constant torment. I never see such men happy. They never enjoy any part of their possessions.

Lionardo: To avoid appearing avaricious, people think they must spend lavishly.

Giannozzo: And to avoid appearing mad, they must be thrifty. But why, with God's help, should one not prefer to be thrifty rather than lavish? Believe me, who have some knowledge and experience of the matter, those great expenditures which are not particularly necessary are not admired by prudent men. I have never seen, or think that you will see, any expenditure so great and lavish or so magnificent but that a multitude of men found in it a multitude of shortcomings. There was always too much of the one thing or too little of the other. You know how it is. If a man plans a dinner, though a dinner is a most proper and civilized kind of expense, almost a sort of tax or tribute to preserve good will and to confirm relationships of friendship, yet, aside from the confusion, worries, and anxieties—this is wanted, that is needed, this other thing also—upheaval and annoyance overwhelm you until you are tired before you have even begun your preparations. Aside from all this there is the throwing away of things, the washing and sweeping all over the house; nothing stays locked, this is lost, this other thing demanded—you seek here, you borrow there, you buy, you spend, you spend some more, you waste. To this just add the regrets, the second thoughts which trouble your mind during the proceedings and afterward as well, an infinite variety of anxieties and troubles that beset you, serious ones, too. And nonetheless, when the smoke is out of the kitchen, the favor you have won by the whole thing is already consumed, all the favor, Lionardo, and you will hardly be noticed for all you have done. If the affair has received some approbation, a few will praise it for some part of its splendor, and many will blame you for the smallness of your largesse. The many, moreover, are right. Any expenditure that is not particularly necessary, it seems to me, can only come from madness. And if a man goes mad in any respect, he ought to go wholly mad in that respect, for to try to be only moderately mad has always been mere double madness and utter folly.

But let all these things go, for they are minor compared with the matters I shall speak of now. These expenditures for the entertainment and due honoring of your friends can only come once or twice a year, and they bear an excellent medicine in themselves for anyone who has tried them once: if he is not wholly out of his mind, I think he will avoid the repetition of them. Lionardo, come to my aid yourself, and think this over a bit. Consider whether there is anything more apt to cause the ruin not only of a family but of a village or a whole community than those—what do they call them in those books of yours, those persons who spend money without reason?

Lionardo: Prodigals.

Giannozzo: Call them what you like. If I had to give them a name, what could I find to call them but "damned pestilence"? Thoroughly off the road themselves, they lead others astray too. Other young men see these prodigals of yours abounding in every sort of entertainment, and since it is the vice of the young to prefer places of delight to the workshop and to seek out spendthrift young companions rather than thrifty old ones, they quickly join them in the consumption of luxuries and delicacies. They live a life of idleness, avoid the kinds of activity men praise, and put their pride and happiness in their power to waste their own resources, neither caring as much for their honor as they ought nor valuing moderation of any kind. True enough, who among them could even hope to become a good man, living in the midst of so many greedy, lying flatterers and besieged by vile and dishonest men, musicians, players, dancers, buffoons, pimps, rubbish dressed in livery and frills? Perhaps this whole crowd does not connive to sit on the doorstep of anyone who is a prodigal, as if at a school and factory of vice, whence the young men used to this kind of life are unable to get out? Oh Lord, what crimes do they not commit, merely to continue in it? They rob their fathers, their relatives, and their friends, they pawn and they sell. Who could tell half the hideous tale? Every day they cause new complaints, every hour brings some fresh infamy; they constantly collect more hate and ill will and enmity and disgrace. Finally, my dear Lionardo, these prodigals are left poor and full of years, without honor and with few, or rather no, friends. Those joyful leeches whom they took for friends in their great days of spending, those lying flatterers who praised their overspending that was their very self-impoverishment and called it a virtue, who, glass in hand, swore and promised to lay down their life—you have seen the water swarming with fish while the bait's afloat; when the bait is gone, all is deserted and empty. I do not want to go on at length on this subject, or give you examples and tell you of all the men I have seen with these very eyes go from great wealth to want through lack of thrift. That, Lionardo, would be a long story—the whole day would not suffice us.

So, to be brief, I shall say only this: as prodigality is evil, so in the same measure is thrift good, valuable, and praiseworthy. Thrift does no one any harm and is good for the family. I tell you, moreover, that I know thrift alone is able to keep you so that you will never suffer need. Thrift is a holy thing, and how many lascivious desires, how many vile longings does it not put from us? Do not doubt it, Lionardo, prodigal and pleasure-seeking youth has ever been inclined to cause the ruin of the family. The old, who are thrifty and modest, are the family's salvation. It is good to be thrifty if only because, in your own mind, you gain the wonderful comfort of knowing that you live very well with what fortune has granted you. The man who lives contentedly with what he possesses does not, in my opinion, merit a name for avarice. It is the spendthrifts, on the contrary, who are truly avaricious, because, since they never tire of spending, they are never content with their gains but seek rapaciously at all times to obtain more money from this source and from that. Yet do not think that I delight in any excessive closefistedness. I say only this much, that the father of a family seems to me unworthy of honor if he is a spendthrift and merely enjoys himself.

Lionardo: If spendthrifts irritate you, Giannozzo, you ought to like those who do not spend. But avarice, which, according to the wise writers, consists in too great a desire for wealth, also consists in not spending.

Giannozzo: What you say is true enough.

Lionardo: Yet you don't like avarice.

Giannozzo: Indeed not.

Lionardo: This thrift you are talking about, then, what sort of thing is it?

Giannozzo: You know, Lionardo, I am not an educated man. I have tried all my life to know things by experience, and not to count much on what others have said. I know what I know more from the actual truth of it than from anyone's persuading me. If one of those people who spend all day reading says to me, "this is how it is," I believe him only if I see a reason for believing it. I like a reason which amounts to a clear demonstration rather than an argument which forces me to admit a point. If another, an uneducated person, gives me the same reason for the same thing, I will believe him without his citing authorities, just as much as I would the man who gives me evidence from a book. I assume the writer of a book was only a man like myself. So, now, perhaps, I shall not be able to answer you in the well-ordered way you would do, since you always spend the day with a book in your hand.

But see here, Lionardo, those spendthrifts of whom I was talking just now I dislike because they spend without reason. The avaricious also irritate me, because they do not make use of their possessions when needed, and because they want wealth too much. You know the sort of man I like? The sort who uses his possessions as the need arises and spends enough, but not more than enough. What is left over he saves, and this is the sort of man I call thrifty.

Lionardo: I see what you mean: those who maintain the mean between too little and too much.

Giannozzo: Yes, yes.

Lionardo: But how do we know what is too much and what is too little?

Giannozzo: Easily, by the ruler in our hand.

Lionardo: I am waiting and hoping to see this ruler.

Giannozzo: This is a simple matter, Lionardo. It can be briefly stated and is most useful to know. With every expenditure one must only be sure that the cost is no greater or heavier or larger than is needed, yet no less than honor requires.

Lionardo: Oh, Giannozzo, how much more help in the things of this world is a man of your wisdom and experience than a scholar without experience.

Giannozzo: What do you mean? Don't you have these things in your books? Yet they say you can find anything in books.

Lionardo: That may be, but I don't remember having seen it anywhere. And if you knew, Giannozzo, how helpful and exactly to our purpose you are proving yourself today, you would be amazed.

Giannozzo: Is that so? I am glad if I can be of any service to you.

Lionardo: The greatest possible service, for these young people here, Battista and Carlo, were hoping to hear some thoughts on the subject of good management, and I was hoping for the same myself. Now from whom could we hear more valuable and more comprehensive ideas on this subject than from you? You are well known among our kinsmen as a man neither so eager to spend as not to be absolutely thrifty nor so thrifty that anyone could ever accuse you of being less than liberal. I want to beg you, therefore, since thrift is such a very useful thing, do not deny us the advantage of learning about it from you. We will listen more faithfully to you than to another, who might teach us avarice rather than thrift. Go on, Giannozzo, and tell us what you think of this holy virtue of thrift. I hope to hear, on what remains of the subject, as on the matters you have already considered, some very distinguished thoughts.

Giannozzo: I would not know how to deny you, Lionardo, for it is you who ask me. It is also my duty to do the things which may give satisfaction to my kinsmen. I tell you more willingly what I know through my own experience of this matter of good management, because you do desire to know and because having listened to me will prove most helpful to you. Your desire to hear me, indeed, is no greater than mine to make you thrifty. I tell you this, thrift has done much for me. If I have any good fortune at all (as at present, thanks be to God, I have middling good fortune), I can say that I have achieved it more by thrift than by any degree of diligence in acquisition. True enough, but sit down. Sit down, Lionardo. These young boys will stand.

Lionardo: I am all right standing.

Giannozzo: Sit down.

Lionardo: You sit. You know the custom of our house, that none of us would ever sit in the presence of his elders.

Giannozzo: Certainly not in public. But these are private talks we have here, and for our own benefit. Sit. It is better to yield in obedience than to insist willfully on what seems to look like better conduct. Sit. Now, what were we saying about thrift? That it was helpful. I don't know your books and what they say about it but I shall tell you what sort of thrift I believe in myself, applied to what things and practiced in what ways. No one, I suppose, has any doubt that thrift is helpful, necessary, honorable, and praiseworthy. What do your books say about it?

Lionardo: What do you suppose, Giannozzo, since as you said those ancient writers were only men like yourself?

Giannozzo: Yes, but more learned ones. And if it were not so, their works would not have lived through so many ages.

Lionardo: I admit that, but it seems to me on these things they say nothing different from what any diligent father of a family observes for himself. What more could they say than you can on things you have seen with your own eyes and know by experience? They say over and over again that if there were no one able to preserve things, it would be folly to bring home what one had earned, and if nothing were being brought in, it would be no less absurd to try to preserve anything.

Giannozzo: Yes. How well they speak! What is the use of earning if there is no thrift? A man exerts himself in the process of acquiring goods in order to have what he needs when he needs it. He provides for sickness in health, as the ant provides for winter in summer. At need, therefore, one must consume; when things are not needed, they should be preserved. And so you have it: all of thrift consists not so much in preserving things as in using them at need. Do you see?

Lionardo: I do indeed, since to fail to use at need would be mere avarice and dishonorable.

Giannozzo: Yes, and poor economy, too.

Lionardo: Poor economy?

Giannozzo: Very poor. Did you ever notice the little old widows? They gather apples and other fruit. They keep them locked up and save them, until the fruit spoils before it is eaten. Then they are always eating the most rotten. In the end all are maggoty and spoiled. Consider: you'll find that all they had to do was throw three or four out of the window, and you could have said they were preserving them by throwing them away. Wouldn't it have been better, foolish old lady, to have thrown those first few away, and to have taken the good ones for your table or to have given some away? This is not preserving, but wasting.

Lionardo: How much better—they might have had some use of them, or at least received some thanks for them.

Giannozzo: Take another example: a drop of rain comes through the roof. The miser waits until tomorrow, and again until the day after tomorrow. It rains again, the miser does not want to spend his money. Again, it rains; the water. And what would have cost a *soldo* costs ten. True?

Lionardo: Often true.

Giannozzo: So you see it is poor economy not to spend money and use things at need. But since thrift consists in using and in preserving things, let us see what things there are to use and to preserve. Now, first of all, I think that to want to use and to preserve the things which belong to someone else would be either presumption or robbery or fraud. Am I right about that?

Lionardo: Very.

Giannozzo: So it is right that the things of which we are truly and carefully thrifty had better be really our own. Now what things are those?

Lionardo: I dare say my wife, my children, my house—those, maybe?

Giannozzo: Oh, those things are not ours, Lionardo. If I can take something from you anytime I like, shall we say that it belongs to you or to me? To you?

Lionardo: I would say it is more yours.

Giannozzo: But fortune can always, at her whim, take your wife, your children, your property, and such?

Lionardo: Certainly she can, yes.

Giannozzo: Then those things belong rather to her than to us. And what do you say of things that cannot be taken from you in any way? Whose are they?

Lionardo: Mine.

Giannozzo: Can the power to love, to desire, to wish, to disdain, and so forth according to your will, can this be taken from you?

Lionardo: Certainly not.

Giannozzo: These things, then, are truly yours.

Lionardo: You speak truly.

Giannozzo: But, to put it in brief, there are three things which a man can truly call his own. They are such that nature gave them to you the day you saw the light, with the freedom to use them well or badly just as it pleased and suited you. These are things nature ordained should always remain with you and never leave you till your last day. One of these things, as you realize, is that moving spirit within us by which we feel desire and anger. Whatever fortune's wish, this remains with us. Another such thing, as you realize, is your body. Nature has made it a vehicle, a kind of cart for moving the spirit about, and nature has commanded that it should never obey any spirit but its own. Thus any animal caged and subjected to others never ceases to try to be free and again to make use of its own self, its wings or feet or other parts, not at another's will but with liberty, at its own behest. Nature hates to have the body escape the guardianship of its spirit, and man, above all, naturally loves liberty. He loves to live at his own command, loves to belong to himself. And this seems to be the general appetite shared by all mortal beings. So these two things are our own, the spirit and the body.

Lionardo: And what is the third?

Giannozzo: Ha! A most precious thing. My very hands and eyes are not so much my own.

Lionardo: Amazing! But what thing is this?

Giannozzo: It cannot be bound, it cannot be diminished. In no way can it be made other than your own, provided you *want* it to be yours.

Lionardo: And at my will it can belong to another?

Giannozzo: And if you wish it can be not yours. Time, my dear Lionardo, time, my children.

Lionardo: No doubt you are right, yet it would not occur to me to call something my own if I could not give it away. Thus it seems to me that I can put all the operations of my spirit at the service of others, so that they would be no longer my own: I could love and hate and be moved at the persuasion of others, desire and not desire, laugh and weep, at the will of another.

Giannozzo: If you were in a boat and floating along with the current in the midst of our river Arno, and if, as sometimes happens to fishermen, you had dirty hands and your face all daubed with mud, would all that water not be yours, if you used it to wash and purify yourself? Right? And, likewise, if you did not use it?

Lionardo: Certainly then it would be not mine.

Giannozzo: That is exactly how it is with time. If a man uses it to wash off the dirt and mud—the ignorance and low desires and vile appetites—that cling to our mind and impure understanding, and if he makes use of time to learn, to think, and to do admirable deeds, he makes time his own. But a man who lets one hour after the other glide by in idleness, never engaging in any worthwhile occupation, certainly loses time. Thus time spent unused is lost, and time well used belongs to him who knows how to use it. Now, my children, you have the actions of the spirit, the body, and time, three things which truly belong to you by nature; and you know how valuable and precious these are. To heal and to care for the body every precious thing is willingly given, and to make the spirit noble, tranquil, and happy, all the desires and longings of the body are suppressed. As to time and how vital it is to the good of the body and the happiness of the spirit, you can consider the matter for yourself and realize that time is a most precious thing. It is of these things that a man ought to be wise and sparing, for they are more our own possessions than any others.

Lionardo: Keep these thoughts in your memory, Battista, and you, too, Carlo. These are not sayings of the philosophers but, like the oracles of Apollo, perfect and holy wisdom such as you will not find in all our books. We are deeply indebted to you, Giannozzo. Proceed.

Giannozzo: I have said that thrift consists in using and in preserving things. It seems to me we must consider these three goods—body, spirit, and time—and see how they may be preserved and also how they may be used. But I intend to be most brief. Listen, then. First, of the spirit, here is how to take proper care of it, Lionardo. I apply it to things that vitally concern myself and my family, and seek to keep it in a state pleasing to God.

Lionardo: What are the things that vitally concern yourself and your family?

Giannozzo: Virtue, kindness, helpfulness. I was not devoted to study when I was young, and that was mainly through my own laziness rather than through lack of talent. My kinsmen, therefore, put me to other work, such as seemed necessary to them in those days. Perhaps they sought profit rather than glory from my gifts. The occupations I then took up I neither knew how nor felt able to abandon. Personally, however, I have always occupied myself in such ways as might win me people's good will, using every means that intelligence and skill could find. Above all, I have always wished to be and to appear good, just, and tranquil, a man who would never irritate or harm others. Neither by my words nor by my deeds did I do anyone any injury, either in his presence or in his absence. These, in truth, are the best activities of the spirit. What I am now doing nearly equals them, teaching what one knows of good, warning those who go astray, offering with all faith and charity to correct them like a father, to counsel with care, in truth and love. Thus I employ my intelligence, energy, and spirit in the service of my own honor and that of my family. There are further activities of the spirit, which I have mentioned above—to love, to hate, to disdain, to hope, to desire, and so on. Again, one must know how to use and how to restrain these—to love the good, to hate the wicked, to disdain the envious, to hope for worthy ends, to desire what is best and noblest.

Lionardo: Devoutly. See Battista and Carlo, how full of pith and marrow are the words Giannozzo speaks. But go on, Giannozzo. Then what is your way of keeping the soul pleasing in the sight of God?

Giannozzo: I have two ways. One is to try and do all I can to keep my spirit joyful. I try never to let my mind be troubled with anger or greed or any other excessive passion. This I have always believed to be an excellent way. The pure and simple spirit, I believe, is the one that pleases God the most. The other way I have of pleasing God, it seems to me, consists in doing nothing of which I am doubtful whether it be good or bad.

Lionardo: Is this enough, do you think?

Giannozo: Yes, I think it is enough, according to what I remember having learned. Eh, my children, do you know why I say never do something about which you are doubtful? Because things that are true and good are luminous and clear in themselves. They are attractive. They appear desirable to us. They are things we want to do. But things that are not good always lie in the shadow of some vile and dirty pleasure, or of some wicked inclination, whatever it may be. They are not things that we truly want to do, but things we ought to flee from. We can follow the light and avoid all shadows. The light of our deeds consists in truth, and spreads by praise and fame. There is nothing in a man's life more shadowy than error and disgrace.

Lionardo: No thrift can ever be more perfect than this thrift which you practice. We are learning today not only true thrift but the way to live well and in a civilized manner. Here is the way to become noble, to live with excellence, to be happy, and to do the things concerning which we are free of any doubt. But, Giannozzo, if it be permitted to ask, did you yourself invent these remarkable and holy precepts or did you, as I thought you said before, learn from others?

Giannozzo: You really like them, do you, my children? Keep them in mind then.

Lionardo: So we shall, for nothing could be more delightful to us or more worthy of being forever remembered.

Giannozzo: When was it now? The year after forty-eight, is that right? No, it was the year after that, in the house of Sir Niccolaio and of Nerozzo, your great uncle, father of your uncle Bernardo, who is both your uncle, Lionardo, and the father of Sir Benedetto and of Francesco, uncle of Bivigliano. These were brothers fathered by Alberto, the brother of Lapo and Neri. Those three were sons of Jacopo the lawyer, who was a son of Sir Benci, another lawyer. The same Lapo was the uncle of Sir Iacopo the knight, and that Sir Iacopo was the brother of our own father, Tomaso. That Jacopo was himself the father of Bishop Paolo, our cousin and the cousin of Sir Cipriano, whose grandson, Sir Alberto, is still alive today. Also that Neri I mentioned, the brother of Lapo and Alberto, was the father of Sir Agnolo. Yes, that's it.

Lionardo: And all that multitude of ancestors of ours whom you just called Sir, were they all really knights, or were they so called only by virtue of age and position?

Giannozzo: They were knights, and very eminent ones, almost all knighted for some particular merit. That Sir Niccolaio of ours, a man of noblest mind and conduct, was one of those who sat as a judge holding the highest place in the administration of justice among the few who ruled the whole republic. He gave to the captain of our troops the standard and banner as he set out against our Pisan foe. This Niccolaio was knighted on the steps of the Signoria, the seat and fort of our government. All our fellow citizens celebrated the occasion and worthily honored all our family. From this foundation and beginning our Alberti family has preserved and increased its dignity and majesty, and has gladly contributed all the labor and expense we could muster. As you know, the first foundations of our public palace were built when Alberto, the son of Sir Iacopo, the lawyer, was a prior in the administration of the republic. Often do I think to myself that from the earliest times to the present there has never been anyone born in our house of Alberti who was not father or son or uncle or grandson of some knighted person of our blood.

Let us pass over this matter of genealogy, however. It is irrelevant to both the subject of thrift, in which we are interested, and the question you raised as to my having developed my own precepts or learned them from others. I wanted to say that in the house of Sir Niccolaio, where Sir Benedetto used to visit, it was ever the custom to talk not about trivial matters but about important questions. These men would discuss in their home what was best for the whole family as well as for the honor and well-being of each member. These were men who constantly read the books of which you are so fond, who were always active in the Palazzo giving counsel to their country, and who talked wherever they might find themselves with men of worth. In discussion they showed their own excellence and improved those who listened to them—that was always their way. For this reason I myself and other young members of our family used to try, as far as our other duties permitted, to remain nearby. We wanted to learn, as well as to show our reverence.

Sometimes at the house of Sir Niccolaio, and sometimes at the homes of the others, there would be a certain old priest, who was white haired, blessed with a pervasive air of modesty and gentleness, had a full, very dignified beard, and expressed in his countenance much goodness and reverence. This man of many excellent thoughts once began to speak of these things there, not of thrift exactly, but of the gifts God gave to us mortals. And he went on to say how much gratitude man owes to God for these great blessings, and how ungrateful a man would prove himself if he failed to take note of, and to make good use of, the grace he had received from God. He declared, however, that nothing properly belongs to us except a certain power of will and force of reason. If anything further could be said to belong to us, it could only be the same three things I spoke of earlier—the spirit, the body, and time. Though the body is subject to many ills, to accidents and to pain, yet, as he explained to us, it does belong to us. When we suffer and overcome our illnesses and troubles with manliness and patience, we achieve no less than when we use our bodies in ways that are happy and joyful.

I would not be able to explain these matters, however, in the wonderful systematic way he could. He expounded at length the question which of these aforesaid three things was truly most entirely the possession of a mortal man. If I remember rightly, he made a great issue of the decision between spirit and time. So we all listened, and he said many things which Messer Benedetto and Messer Niccolaio admitted they had never heard before. I myself liked this old man so much that I gave him my rapt and fixed attention while he spoke for several hours, and I never grew weary. I have never forgotten his weighty thoughts. The noble quality of his manner, too, has remained with me forever. Even now I seem to see him before me, modest, gracious, calm, and unruffled in discussion. Then, as you see, I appropriated for myself certain ideas of his which I remembered, and I made them part of my philosophy of life.

Lionardo: May God reward that old man and bless you for having so well passed on his teaching to us. Now, however, since this is the order of your argument, having spoken of the spirit, would you tell us something of the management of the body?

Giannozzo: It is noble and valuable work, and similar to the management of the spirit. I keep my body active in honorable ways. I engage in as noble and useful activities as I can find. I have tried to keep my body healthy, strong, and beautiful for a long time. I keep myself neat, clean, and well groomed. I take care above all to use my hands, my tongue, and every member as I do my intelligence and all that is mine in the service of the honor and fame of my country, my family, and myself. At all times I strive toward ends both practical and honorable.

Lionardo: You have certainly earned our thanks and our admiration, for, with these words, you remind us to model ourselves on your own example. But what, Giannozzo, have you found most helpful in the preservation of health? I shall believe your answer, for I have never seen, I think, an old man as fresh, as straight, and altogether as handsome as you. Your voice, your vision, and all your sinews are pure and whole and unencumbered. This is an all too marvelous and rare thing at your age.

Giannozzo: Heh, thank God I do feel quite well and healthy, though less vigorous than I used to be. But it isn't vigor a man needs at my age so much as prudence and discretion. I do wish I could at least walk as I used to do. No doubt about it, just on account of this lack of vigor, I often leave undone things which it would be well for myself and for my friends to get done. I cannot be as zealous in caring for my friends' concerns as I would be for my own. But, though I thank God, still I also feel it is partly by my own merit that at my age I am freer from ailments and less hampered by infirmity than many younger men. Health in an old man is generally a sign of continence in youth. It is important to take care of one's health at every age by exercising some caution, and more care is required to guard the more advanced years. We ought to be extremely watchful in the management of so precious a commodity as health.

Lionardo: This I admit is the way to manage health wisely. But what do you find are the most practical means to health?

Giannozzo: Exercise in moderate and pleasant form.

Lionardo: And what else?

Giannozzo: Exercise in pleasant form.

Lionardo: And after that?

Giannozzo: Exercise, my dear Lionardo, exercise, my dear children— this was ever the watchman and the doctor of health.

Lionardo: And what if one does not get much exercise?

Giannozzo: It is rarely indeed that I find I cannot manage to take some form of exercise, but when it does happen that other occupations cause me to exercise less than I usually do, I find that a well-controlled diet is good. Don't eat when not hungry, don't drink when not thirsty. For my own purposes this is what I have discovered: hard as some foods may be to digest, and old as I am, there is usually nothing that I cannot digest within twenty-four hours. This is the best rule for you, my children, and it is brief as well as correct: find out by careful attention what is bad for you, and avoid it; learn what is good for you, and be sure to obtain it.

Lionardo: All right. Cleanliness, then exercise, diet, and the avoidance of their opposites keep up our health.

Giannozzo: And our youth and beauty, too. The difference between old and young, after all, I think consists in this: the one is weak, the other strong, the one fresh, the other flaccid and shriveled. If a man preserves his health, therefore, he also preserves his strength and youth and good looks. Good looks, in my opinion, are largely a question of good color and a fresh complexion, and nothing is so salutary for the blood or keeps one's color up like a combination of exercise and temperance.

Lionardo: Now you have told us of the management of both spirit and body. There remains the matter of time. And how, Giannozzo, do you economize with time? Time unceasingly escapes us, and there is no way of preserving it.

Giannozzo: Did I not say that thrift consists as much in making good use of things as in preserving them? My plan, therefore, is to make as good use as possible of time, and never to waste any. I use time as much as possible on praiseworthy pursuits. I do not spend my time on base concerns. I spend no more time on anything than is needed to do it well.

And to waste no part of such a precious thing, I have a rule that I always follow: never remain idle. I avoid sleep, and I do not lie down unless overcome by weariness, for it seems disgraceful to me to fall without fighting or to lie beaten—in short, like so many people, to take an attitude of defeat sooner than enter the battle. This then is what I do: I avoid sleep and idleness, and I am always doing something. To be sure that one pursuit does not crowd out another, and that I don't find I have started several things but completed none, or perhaps have done only the less important and left the best undone, do you know, my children, what I do? First thing in the morning, when I arise, I think to myself, "What are the things I have to do today?" There are a certain number of things, and I run through them, consider, and assign to each some part of my time: this for the morning, this later today, and that this evening. In this way I find every task gets done in an orderly way, almost without effort.

Messer Niccolaio Alberti, who was himself a most active and energetic individual, used to remark that he never saw a diligent man walk along at any but a leisurely pace. It may seem paradoxical, but in my own case he spoke the truth. The man who neglects things finds that his time escapes him. Then necessity or at least desire brings him to action. Having, by then, almost let the season go by, he must act in a mad rush. With strenuous effort he accomplishes the same thing that earlier and at the proper time would have been easy. Remember, my children, that there is never such an abundance of anything, or such ease in obtaining it, but that it becomes difficult to find out of season. For seeds and plants and grafting, for flowers, fruits, and everything else, there is a season: out of season the same thing can be arranged only with a great deal of trouble. One must, therefore, keep an eye on time, and plan to suit the season; one must labor steadily, and not lose a single hour. I could tell you how precious a thing is time, but it will have to be said elsewhere, with more polished style, more brilliance, and greater learning than mine. Just remember not to waste time.

Do as I do. In the morning I plan my whole day, during the day I follow my plan, and in the evening, before I retire, I think over again what I have done during the day. Then, if I was careless in performing some task, and can repair the damage immediately, I do so; for I would sooner lose sleep than lose time, that is, than let the right moment for doing something slip by. Sleep, food, and things of that sort I can catch up on tomorrow, and take care of my needs, but the moment for doing something that must be done, no. Though it happens rarely to me—if I have arranged my tasks well with a time assigned for each, have planned a good order, and have not been negligent in carrying it out—it rarely or almost never happens to me that I must give up or postpone some necessity. If it does happen, however, and it is too late to change the situation, I view this as a lesson so that I shall not let time get away from me like that again.

So I manage these three things as you have been hearing. I employ the spirit and the body and time in ways only that are good. I try to preserve them adequately, and I take care not to waste them at all. In this I expend much care and I try to be as watchful and as effective as I can, for it seems to me these are the most precious things there are, and much more truly mine than any others. Riches, power, government—these are the possessions not of men, no, but of fortune—yes. To men they belong only insofar as fortune grants them their use.

Lionardo: But what of these things which you enjoy by fortune's favor, do you try to manage them with thrift?

Giannozzo: Dear Lionardo, it would be negligence and folly not to try to manage anything which, by our use of it, becomes our own. For fortune's gifts are ours only with her favor and, second, only insofar as we know how to use them. Though the truth is that in these terrible days fortune so cruelly opposes us Albertis—she does not give us kindly or generously of what is hers, but rather tries wickedly and spitefully to trouble even those things that are ours—that we hardly find occasion to practice wise management. We have always hoped, in this exile of ours, to return again to our own country, to come together again in our own house, and to rest among our kinsmen. This hope and longing have grown more fervent, indeed, as we continually suffer and decline while unable to settle our spirits or to root our lives in some kind of stable order. Had I been able from the beginning to imagine—I shall not say to know—what misfortunes, how much misery, and for how long our Alberti family would suffer, if I could have believed, when I was a young man, that I should someday be what I now am, an old man grown gray far from his home, perhaps, my children, I would have done things differently.

Lionardo: Yet, says Battista here, remember the teaching of that Terentian character, Demiphus. Every man finds it hard in prosperity to envisage how in time of need he will sustain the cruel tyranny of fortune and the dangers, injury, and exile that may come. When you return from a journey, therefore, think of some misdeed that children or wife may have committed or of some accident that may have befallen them, for these things happen every day—thus your spirit will never be overwhelmed by some unexpected calamity. The sword a man has seen ahead of time usually strikes less deep. Also, if you find things safe and better than you had imagined, you will count all that as gain. If this is a good rule to follow in prosperity, how much more so when things are on the decline and falling apart.

Giannozzo: Ah, my dear Lionardo, how could I have supposed that others would be more vengeful in our time of troubles than I myself? How, my children, should I have thought that those who, for some reason, had dishonorably or for slight cause gravely offended our family would persist more obstinately in their rancor and hate than we, who daily suffer the effects of their attacks and depredations? Yet I am one of those who for years now has canceled out the name and record in his heart of the ones who caused us so much unjust grief lasting even to the present. Never, it seems to me, did any man so harden his heart as these monstrous and cruel persons, who expelled us unjustly and persecute us unmercifully. Nor are they content to keep us living in miserable circumstances. They still reward anyone who increases our sufferings in any way. But let God be our judge in this quarrel, a judge more merciful than severe toward the sinner. My children, I still say it would have been a good thing for me had I taken a different view of our lot many years ago.

Lionardo: What would you have done then? How would you have planned for a life of thrift and temperance?

Giannozzo: Very well—my life might have been a tranquil one, free of any serious worries. I would have considered as follows: "Come now, Giannozzo, tell me, what has fortune granted you?" And I would have realized that she gave me a family and certain possessions within my house, true? Anything else? Yes. What? Honor and friendship outside my house.

Lionardo: Do you, by any chance, use the word honor [*onore*] as some of our fellow citizens do, to signify holding public office and being in the government?

Giannozzo: Far from it, my dear Lionardo, far from it, my dear children. There is nothing I think which a man should consider further from enhancing his honor than his participation in all these governments. And do you know why, my children? Partly because we Albertis are excluded from those murky waters now, and partly because I never thought well of them anyway. I always have thought any other way of life preferable to that of all these public men, as we might call them. Who can help being repelled by such a life? A life of worries, anxieties, and burdens, a life of servitude.

What is there to distinguish those who work in governments from mere public servants? You construct here, appeal there, bow before one man, quarrel with another, insult a third; many suspicions and a thousand grudges, innumerable enmities, no true friendships, but plenty of promises and abundant offers, all full of pretence, vanity, and lies. And the greater your need, the less likely you are to find anyone who will keep his promises or prove faithful. Thus it is that all your labors and all your hopes can break down at one stroke, with suffering and grief for you and the ruin of your estate. Should you succeed, however, by infinite prayers, in obtaining some good fortune, what have you gained? There you are, seated in office. What does your advantage there consist of but this: you can now steal and use violence with some degree of liberty.

You hear constant complaints, innumerable accusations, great disturbances, and you are personally beset by litigants, avaricious creatures, and men of the grossest injustice who fill your ears with suspicions, your soul with greed, your mind with fear and trouble. You are obliged to ignore your own concerns in order to untangle the folly of other men. Now you must organize taxes, now expenditures, now provide for wars, now clarify and revise laws; there are always so many connections between various tasks and activities of government that neither you alone nor you with the help of supporters can ever accomplish as much as you want. Everyone considers his own aims honorable and his own judgment admirable, his own opinion better than any. Whether you follow popular thought in its errors or rely on the arrogance of a leader, you are disgraced as though the mistake were your own; even if you labor to serve others, when you please one you displease a hundred. What a madness, though unrecognized, what an affliction, though men do not shun it, an evil which, inspite of its consequences, is not generally detested—and this, I suppose, only because this one form of servitude is somehow thought to bestow a kind of glory. The madness of men—who think so much of going heralded by trumpets and with staff in hand—is that they abandon domestic tranquillity and true peace of mind.

Madness, vanity, pride, and tyranny—what excuses are made here for wickedness! If you cannot bear to have men who, though less rich than you, are perhaps of more ancient lineage considered as your equals, which they are, you seek power. You cannot live without oppressing the weak, and so you seek power. And to have power, what do you, in your folly, do? Maniacs, you rush into every danger, you risk death. Brutes, you call it honor to be encircled by vice-ridden men and not to know how to live with good ones; it suits you to serve and to be allied with all the thieves, with men whose condition is so vile that they care little if they risk their lives in the service of your cause. You call it honor to be among robbers, honor to appease, to feed, and to serve men of servile state—brutes.

You deserve to be hated if you enjoy the perversion of moral life and endless travail which overwhelms those who fill public offices and administrative functions. What can be the inward delight of a man whose ears are assailed by complaints, grief, the weeping of orphans and widows and of victims of disaster and destitution—what delight, if he be not, in fact, a fierce and brutish creature? What sort of man is content to confront all day long and to live always among a thousand bands of scoundrels, embezzlers, spies, scandalmongers, robbers, and criminals practicing every sort of fraud and immorality? What sort of recreation is it, as a butcher and render of the human body, to go every evening and twist a man's arms and legs, hear him cry with anguished voice for mercy, and still resort to further horrible tortures. A disgusting thing even to contemplate, a thing to avoid at all costs. Yet, cruel creatures, you desire to govern?

Certainly you will say yes, for I think it is a noble deed to suffer such burdens in order to punish the wicked and to raise and reward the good. So to punish wicked men you must first become worse? I think no man is good if he cannot live contented with his own. The man who covets and seeks the goods of others, I think, is worse. And worst is he who thirsts after and usurps the public wealth. I don't blame you if, after you display great excellence and enjoy great fame, your country calls on you and imposes a part of its burdens on you. I call it an honor to be thus entreated by your fellow citizens. But that I should do as many do, cast myself at the feet of this or that important person, make up the tail of some man's procession, seek by serving to become a commander of others, that, indeed, I should lend my hand to doing harm and disservice to someone in order to suit someone else whose favor I need in order to climb to power, that I should wish, as almost all of them do, to inscribe my name in the rolls of state almost as a way of making money, as if it were my store, treating the state as if it were to be the dowry of my daughters, that I should in any way make private what is public and use for gain what my country grants me as an honor, making my country my prey—no, my dear Lionardo, no, my dear children, no.

A man wants to live for himself, not for the community. He is willing to be asked for help by his friends, true, where this does not mean that you neglect your own concerns and where it does not lead to serious losses for you. A man is no friend of mine if he does not avoid doing what would lead to my injury or shame. One is willing to leave part of one's own affairs for the sake of friends, if you then receive in return, not necessarily a reward, but good feeling and gratitude. That is how, you know, men have always been happiest, following the middle of the road.

You who have read many histories could give more examples than I to show that this is so. The histories will all confirm that no one ever fell to ruin who had not first climbed too high. As for me, let it suffice me to be and to appear good and just. As long as that is my state I can never be truly disgraced. That honor [*onoranza*] alone is mine even in exile, and it will remain with me as long as I do not abandon it. Let others enjoy pomp, and let the winds blow wide their sails while fortune wills. They delight in their power, but they sorrow when they do not have it. They weep when they fear they must lose it; they grieve having lost it. To us who are content with what is ours and never desire what belongs to others, meanwhile, it will never be a source of regret not to possess what is public or to lose what we have never prized. Who, in any case, could value those obligations, labors, and innumerable pangs of spirit? My children, let us stand on the plain, trying only to be good and just householders. Let us delight in our excellent family. Let us delight in those goods fortune bestows on us, sharing them with our friends. A man is highly enough honored when he lives untainted by vice and untouched by shame.

Lionardo: If I understand you rightly, Giannozzo, yours is that magnificent and noble spirited will which has always seemed to me greater and more worthy of a manly temper than any other aspiration or desire of mortal man. I see that your first aim is self-sufficiency, a worthy resolve and proper to a princely spirit, to live with no need of anyone else, to be contented with what fortune grants us. There are some, whom I feel you justly reproach, who think it greatness and breadth of spirit to undertake everything hard and difficult, every sort of toilsome and painful labor in order to gain more power than other citizens. There are quite a few such men in our own country as well as in other states. Having been raised in the most ancient liberty of our city and being filled with bitterest hate against any kind of tyrant, they are not satisfied with the common liberty of all, but want more liberty and license than anyone else. Certainly, Giannozzo, if a man takes it into his head to want a place among the magistrates who guide public affairs, not because he wishes and hopes to merit the praises and the gratitude of good men but because he longs with a single, immoderate appetite to rule and be obeyed, I agree such a man is much to be condemned. He will, as you say, prove himself anything but a good citizen.

Like you, I would say that a good citizen loves tranquillity, but not so much his own tranquillity as that of other good men. He rejoices in his private leisure, but does not care less about that of his fellow citizens than about his own. He desires the unity, calm, peace, and tranquillity of his own house, but much more those of the country and of the republic. These good things, moreover, cannot be preserved if men of wealth or wisdom or nobility among the citizens seek more power than the other citizens, who are also free but less fortunate. Yet neither can these same republics be preserved if all the good men are solely content with their private leisure. Wise men say that good citizens should undertake to care for the republic and to toil at the tasks of their country, not shaken by the follies of men, in order to further the public peace and preserve the general good. Thus they also avoid giving a place of power to the wicked, who through the indifference of the good and through their own dishonest wish soon pervert every plan and undermine both public and private well-being.

So you see, Giannozzo, that the admirable resolve which would make private honor one's sole rule in life, though noble and generous in itself, may still be not the proper guide for spirits eager to seek glory. Fame is born not in the midst of private peace but in public action. Glory springs up in public squares; reputation is nourished by the voice and judgment of many persons of honor, and in the midst of the people. Fame flees from every solitary and private spot to dwell gladly in the arena, where crowds are gathered and celebrity is found; there the name is bright and luminous of one who with hard sweat and assiduous toil for noble ends has projected himself up out of silence and darkness, ignorance, and vice. For these reasons I have never felt that one should object to a man's seeking by means of praiseworthy works and studies, but no less by a devout and careful adherence to good conduct, to gain the favor of some honorable and well-established citizen. I would not call it servitude to do my duty; there is no doubt, however, that it has always been the duty of young men to respect their elders and eagerly to seek among them for the same fame and dignity by which the elders themselves enjoy love and reverence. Nor would I call it power lust if a man shows much care and interest in doing hard and generous things, for these are the way to honor and glory. It may be because there is now in our country no public official but seems to you distempered of mind and servile of spirit that you thus severely condemn anyone who would want to be inscribed in that number, among not good but rather the vilest citizens.

Yet this is my own longing, Giannozzo, so much so that if I might earn fame and favor and reputation, and stand honored, loved, adorned with dignity and the respect of my fellow citizens in my own country, I would never shun this, Giannozzo, nor be afraid of the enmity I might incur from some citizen who was baneful and wicked. Even where it was necessary to deal with men, sometimes with fatal severity, I would esteem this a pious act, to root out and destroy thieves and all scoundrels and to extinguish every last flame of lawless greed, even among my own relatives. As this is not open to us, for the present, however, let us cease to pursue it; I do not say with you that it is worthless, for I continue to esteem honor and fame above any other of the blessings of fortune. Let us not pursue with our longings, however, what the force of circumstances makes inaccessible to our exertions. Let us go by your teaching and await the season when, perhaps, our patience and moderation will receive some recompense. Then the injustice and spite of ill-willed, intemperate enemies who still exceed all bounds in their insults and cruelties toward us will perhaps, by God's justice, be rewarded with some fair and well-earned vengeance. In our present situation, Battista and Carlo, let us merely attempt to earn some praise and fame by our excellence, zeal, and skill, and so prepare ourselves to be of service to the republic, to our country. When the time comes, then, we may prove ourselves such men that Giannozzo and other most wise and moderate elders may not deem us unworthy to receive the honor of a high place in public life.

Giannozzo: Thus would I have you do, my children. Thus do I hope and expect you will do, and thus shall you gain and maintain a name of some distinction. But let me impress upon you once more that one must never—I do not say for honor's sake, for indeed honor may lead one to give up many things, but for the sake of ruling others—never cease to bear rule over oneself. Do not abandon your private concerns to guide public affairs. I remind you of this, for if a man finds he has less than he needs in his home, he will find still less outside; nor will the public power he has redeem his private necessity. Public honors will not feed the family. Be as careful and diligent in fulfilling your domestic charges as you must be, but to public matters give, not whatever ambition and pride might suggest but what your conscience and the gratitude of your fellow citizens dictate.

Lionardo: You give us a clear idea, Giannozzo, of what we ought to do. And so we shall. Tell us, however, you have named four private and domestic needs: family and wealth within the house, honor and friendship outside it—now which of these is dearest to your heart?

Giannozzo: By nature, love and piety make the family dearest of all to me. And to govern the family you must have possessions; and to preserve the family and your possessions, friends are necessary. With them you may take counsel when you must avoid or else successfully endure adversity. And to enjoy possessions, family, and friendship with your friends, it is necessary to hold some position and to exercise honorable authority.

Lionardo: What do you mean by family?

Giannozzo: Children, wife, and other members of the household, both relatives and servants.

Lionardo: I understand.

Giannozzo: And do you know how to apply our system of good management to them? No differently than to ourselves: we shall employ them in honorable ways, put them to virtuous and valuable tasks, keep them healthy and contented, and see that no one wastes his time. And do you know how to be sure no one is wasting his time?

Lionardo: Be sure each of them is busy?

Giannozzo: Not good enough. Rather, be sure each of them is doing what it is his business to do. See that the lady is watching over the children, seeing to the provisions, supervising the household, that the children are at work on their studies, that the others are trying diligently and well to do what their superiors tell them. And do you know, on the other hand, how they would be merely wasting time?

Lionardo: Doing nothing, I suppose.

Giannozzo: Certainly, and also if what one could do is occupying two or more; or if, where two or more are needed, one is toiling and sweating all alone; or if one or more are given tasks for which they are useless or ill suited. Where too many are employed, some are wasted. Where there are fewer than needed or where the workers are not sufficiently skilled for the job, it is worse than if they did nothing, since they labor in vain and largely upset or spoil the thing they are set to do.

Lionardo: Well said.

Giannozzo: Certainly they should not be allowed to waste their time like this. Each should be ordered to do what he knows how to do and can do. To be sure, moreover, that each one can and will act with diligence and love in the position assigned to him, let them follow the same system I do in performing my own task. My job is to make just demands on my family, to teach them diligent and good work, and to give to each what is needed and proper for the task. Do you know how I go about my job to do it better? First, I think for a long, long while about what I could use and what is best, then I go about obtaining it, and endure hardship in order to have it, then I preserve it with care, and finally I teach my household to take care in keeping it for its proper use and then in using it.

Lionardo: Do you take just so much of things as you think you will need and no more?

Giannozzo: Always somewhat more, so that if some is spilled or spoiled or lost, there will not be less than needed.

Lionardo: And if something is left over?

Giannozzo: I decide which is better, to offer it to a friend who can use it or, after all, to keep it for the family's use, for there should not be the least insufficiency of anything required in the family. I have always wished to have in my house all the things that my family found useful or necessary.

Lionardo: And what do you, Giannozzo, think that a family requires?

Giannozzo: Many things, my dear Lionardo, good fortune and much that men cannot control.

Lionardo: But the things men can control, what are they?

Giannozzo: Those are, to provide a house where all your flock can gather, to provide food for them, and to give them clothes to wear.

Lionardo: And to make them good and well brought up?

Giannozzo: Indeed, nothing is more vital to the family, in my opinion, than to educate the youth to be well behaved and to have excellent character. But it is not part of our present discussion of the household to consider the raising of children.

Lionardo: And those other matters, how do you manage them?

Giannozzo: I have told you already that in these calamitous days, I am not in a position to be a truly thrifty householder.

Lionardo: So you did say, yet I know you have a big family and you want them all to be honorable and temperate as you are yourself, and so you live in a companionable and fine way together in your house. That is why I ask you how you order these matters.

Giannozzo: As well as I can, given the times and the adverse circumstances.

Lionardo: But, that we may hear your full teaching, suppose that you were of my age, had a wife and children, were also prudent and as experienced as you are, and altogether determined to maintain a well-run household. How would you arrange things?

Giannozzo: Oh, my son, if I were your age, I could do many things which, at present, I cannot and therefore do not do. My first concern would be to select my house where I could remain as long as I wished, living in comfort and having no need to move. It is unbelievable, my dear Lionardo, and, not having the experience, you may not altogether believe me, how much trouble and expense, how much discomfort and irritation accompanies a move from place to place. Things are lost, misplaced, and broken. In addition there are the anxieties with which your mind is afflicted when spirit and thought are distracted and disrupted, and it is a long time before you are once again well settled. As to the expenses that grow out of settling yourself in a new house, I shall say nothing. This is why it is essential to find, from the start, a place as convenient and suitable as I was saying.

Lionardo: Alas, dear Giannozzo, we who are still young and who were either born in exile or raised in the lands of others are no longer ignorant of the troubles and toil involved in moving. Our cruel fortune casts us hither and thither from day to day and never gives us peace. We are her victims, and she is ever on our trail, ever wounding, even overwhelming us with new calamities more terrible than the old. But let us thank God, who thus provides us with the opportunity to gain no little honor by our infinite patience in the face of evil and by our rare, marvelous, indeed incredible faithfulness amid adversity. Back to our subject, now, however. I ask you, Giannozzo, what would you do to find a place of lasting repose, and that in the lands of others?

Giannozzo: I would look for the sort of land best suited to give me just such repose, from which I would not have to move and where I might live without inconvenience and with honor.

Lionardo: But what criteria would you apply to find the country suitable for your purposes? Wouldn't it be difficult not only to know what it should be like but also to find it?

Giannozzo: Not at all. It would certainly not be very hard for me, my dear Lionardo, and you shall see why. First, I would find out how good, how healthy life was in that spot. I would look mainly at the young people and the children—if they were fresh and handsome I would assume the air was good and healthy, for childhood is very susceptible and sensitive to the kind of air and to things harmful to health. And if there were also many old people there in a thriving, upright, vigorous state, I would suppose that I, too, might grow old there. Then, next, I would look at the neighboring lands and the neighbors to see whether this were an area open or protected in case of foreign invasions, and I would note whether the place were fertile in itself or whether it depended on many resources brought from outside. I would also discover by what means these outside things came in and whether, in case of sudden need, the emergency could be quickly and easily met. I would investigate to learn whether the neighbors were helpful or harmful, and I would ask about other troubles, such as plague and pestilence, and consider whether, in case of need, I could withdraw to that place without great expense.

Above all, I would look closely and diligently into the matter of the character of the people who lived there, whether they were rich and honorable persons, and learn whether the region had a good and stable government, just laws, and moderate leaders. For, my children, if a land is justly ordered and governed with wisdom, it will never suffer the attacks of enemies or evil fortune or the wrath of God. It will have neighbors who are well disposed, peaceful conditions, and a stable government. If the citizens are honorable and wealthy, they will have no desire to rob others, rather they will help the industrious and honor the good.

Lionardo: But where could one ever find such a country, one so entirely praiseworthy in its ways? I certainly think it would be hard to find unless, indeed, you who love to live in Venice think that that one land is less corrupt than any other in all these respects.

Giannozzo: And yet I would look for it. I should not like to have to regret my failure to try. And I would settle down in the country I found did have the most and the most important of these qualities.

Lionardo: Which are most important?

Giannozzo: Listen, my dear Lionardo, it seems to me a matter of no slight difficulty to try to find the most important among them, but though I do not know for certain, I shall say freely what occurs to me just as it comes to mind. Among all the conditions, health seems to me primary; therefore I would particularly search for a place where the air and other features of the country were good for the health. A healthy man, as you know, my children, is going to earn his living somehow anywhere, and if he is just and good, everyone will respect him.

Lionardo: And give him honor?

Giannozzo: My dear Lionardo, a man who is good and who knows how to make it apparent to others that he is good will be honored and esteemed anywhere.

Lionardo: I am satisfied. But first, what conditions do you find most conducive to health?

Giannozzo: The most important condition is the thing you must use just as you find it, like it or not: the air.

Lionardo: And after that?

Giannozzo: Other good things required for our food and nourishment, and particularly good wine. You are laughing, Lionardo.

Lionardo: And where would you settle, then?

Giannozzo: Where I could stay in tranquillity and was looked upon with favor.

Lionardo: What would you do, buy your house or rent one?

Giannozzo: Definitely not rent, for in the course of time a man finds he has bought his house several times over and still does not own it. I would, furthermore, buy a house that was airy, spacious, and suited to hold my family and if a good friend should come by to offer him good lodging too. And for this purpose I would try to spend a minimum.

Lionardo: Would you perhaps choose an out of the way house, where they sold cheap or, as they say, at bargain prices?

Giannozzo: Don't call that a bargain. No price is good when you pay it for something that does not suit you. I would try to spend money on a house that would do for me, and not pay more than it was worth. I would not be impetuous about it or show myself an eager buyer. I would choose a house in a good neighborhood and in a well-known street, where honorable citizens lived with whom I could safely make friends, and with whose wives my wife could enjoy honorable and wholly blameless companionship. I would also inquire carefully about who had lived there in previous times, and ask how healthy and fortunate they had been. There are certain houses in which no one ever seems to have been able to live happily.

Lionardo: Yes, indeed, how true. I recall one beautiful and magnificent room of which I have observed the story. Some grew poor there, another was left all alone, another was expelled in disgrace, all reached such straits as to suffer grief. Your thought is truly excellent, to take a suitable house in a good and honorable neighborhood, in a justly governed, wealthy, and peaceful healthy country where good things abound. And then, Giannozzo, when you have fulfilled these conditions, how do you manage the rest of your household economy?

Giannozzo: I would want all my family to live under one roof, to warm themselves at one hearth, and to seat themselves at one table.

Lionardo: For your greater comfort, I suppose; not to live in solitude, to be the father in their midst, surrounded every evening, loved, revered, the guardian and teacher of all the youth, a state which is generally the greatest satisfaction in the life of older people.

Giannozzo: A very great satisfaction. And also, my dear Lionardo, it is more economical, my dear children, to live thus enclosed behind a single door.

Lionardo: Is that so?

Giannozzo: Yes, and I shall convince you of it. Tell me, Lionardo, if it were night right now and dark and there burned a torch here in the middle of this place, you and I and these others would all be able to see enough to read, write, and do what we liked, is that not right? And if we were to separate, you over there, I upstairs, the boys elsewhere, and all wanted as much light as before to see by, do you think the pieces of this same torch which we might have shared out among ourselves would burn as long a time as the whole torch in one piece would have?

Lionardo: Certainly less long. Who could deny that? After all, the wood burned before from one spot, now from three.

Giannozzo: And now suppose it were very cold and we had many logs burning here. If you wanted your share of them elsewhere, and these boys took their part to still another spot, do you think you would keep warm better or less well?

Lionardo: Less well.

Giannozzo: Thus it is with the family. Many things are sufficient when unbroken that are insufficient when taken to pieces and widely separated. A different warmth will a man feel from one of his own fellow citizens than among strangers, and a different light of prestige and authority will emanate from one who is accompanied by his own people, whom there are many reasons to trust and many reasons to fear, than from one who walks with a few strangers or without company. The father of a family followed by many of his kinsmen will be more eminent than one who is alone and seems abandoned. Now let me talk to you like the practical rather than literary man that I am, and give you the kind of reasons and examples that are in my mind. I understand this, that at two tables, two tablecloths are spread, two hearths consume two piles of logs, two households need two servants, while one can do with one. But I don't know how to explain well to you what I think; yet I feel I am telling you the truth. To make two families out of one requires double expense, and many things happen that it is easier to judge of by experience than by talk, easier to feel than to explain. Indeed, I am not pleased with this dividing of families, this going in and out of separate entrances, nor has my spirit ever suffered Antonio, my brother, to live under a different roof than my own.

Lionardo: That is admirable.

Giannozzo: Yes, my dear Lionardo, families are to be gathered under a single roof, and if, when the family has grown, a single room no longer holds them, at least let them all repose in the shadow of a single will.

Lionardo: Words worthy of the great authority you enjoy. I take note of this and shall keep it forever in memory. Let families remain united in will. And then, Giannozzo, when everyone is in the house, would they all ask to dine?

Giannozzo: True enough. Then let lunch and dinner be served them, my dear Lionardo, at the right times and of good kind.

Lionardo: Good dining? Shall I take that to mean eating good things?

Giannozzo: Good, yes, my dear Lionardo, and abundant too. Not pheasant and capon and partridge or other delicacies such as are prepared for the sick, but let there be a proper table for good citizens, so that no well-disposed member of your family would want to eat elsewhere in hopes of assuaging hunger better than at home. Let your table be a good domestic spread, with no lack of wine and plenty of bread. Let the wine be pure and the bread, too, good enough, and let there be fine and sufficient condiments for the bread.

Lionardo: Good. And would you buy these things, Giannozzo, from day to day?

Giannozzo: No, I would not buy them; that would not be thrifty.

When a man sells things do you think he will let out of the house what is best or rather what is worst?

Lionardo: The worst, and what they think they cannot well preserve. But things that are good and useful are also sold, because of the need for money.

Giannozzo: This I admit. But if a man be wise, he will first sell the worser sort. And when he does sell the better, does he not attempt to sell higher than it came to him? Does he not try with every trick to make it seem better than it is?

Lionardo: Often.

Giannozzo: So you see, the buyer spends that surplus, and he runs the risk of finding he has been duped, drawing something of poor durability or low quality. Right? And even aside from other reasons, to me it means better value to possess all that I need ready at hand and to have tried out my crops over the years so that I know their seasons of perfection, rather than to go looking for things elsewhere.

Lionardo: Would you perhaps wish to have in your house all that you will need in your domestic stores for the whole year?

Giannozzo: Yes, I would like to have in the house whatever can be kept there without danger or great effort and whatever can be well preserved. And what I cannot keep well except by taking great trouble and using too much space in the house, that I would choose to sell and then reprovide for myself in due time, for I would rather suit myself to the season and leave the labor, trouble, and danger to others.

Lionardo: Would you sell what you had first bought?

Giannozzo: As fast as I could if keeping it caused me loss. But if possible I would prefer not to have to sell or to buy now this and now that. These are tasks for merchants and are low preoccupations. It is better thrift really to avoid such concerns—better to spend a bit extra on something and give your attention to matters of more moment. But the best thrift of all, I think, is altogether to provide for things on time. And I tell you this further thing, I would like not to have to remove some money every year from my supply of cash.

Lionardo: I don't see how that can be.

Giannozzo: I shall tell you how. I would make every effort to have estates from which my house could be kept furnished with grain, wine, wood, and straw—all much more cheaply than by purchase in the market. I would there raise flocks, pigeons, chickens, and fish as well.

Lionardo: I agree entirely with your view, Giannozzo, but I have doubts on one point: can it be true economy to establish these undertakings on the land of others; for your farm is useful to the family and apt to win the favor of the landlord, yet I fear you will always find the owner recalling it in order to enjoy it himself and exploit the great improvements which you have added at your own expense and by your own labor. And if you do not make such expenditures, the farm will not, I think, be such as you want to raise food for your family. Truly wise husbandmen can hardly praise, I think, your paying workers anew day by day and giving them a salary and lending them the necessary tools, and then, when you value their work and services and want them again, losing them through a change of lands.

Giannozzo: For this very reason, and for others too, I would buy my land with my own money, so that it might belong to me and to my children and then to my grandchildren, so that I would see to its management and cultivation with more love and so that my own people, remaining there through the passage of time, would gain the fruit of the plants and the work I had put into it.

Lionardo: Would you want fields which were all together in one place to yield the different crops and fruits you have mentioned: grain, wine, olives, straw, and wood?

Giannozzo: I would if I could.

Lionardo: But tell me something, Giannozzo. To grow good wine one needs steep slopes and sunshine; for good grain you need the open plain with light and loamy ground; good wood is found on well-watered mountain ridges; hay where it is moist and swampy. How would you obtain such diverse conditions in a single place? Tell me Giannozzo, do you think that there are many places to be found equally suited for grapes and grain and woods and pasture? And if you found them, do you think you could have them for less than a staggering price?

Giannozzo: Certainly they exist—and how many! My dear Lionardo, I remember in Florence how many such places there were aside from the estates we had, the place of Messer Benedetto, and those of Messer Niccolaio and those of Messer Cipriano and those of Messer Antonio and of our other Albertis—estates which left nothing to be desired, situated in purest air, in lovely country, with a beautiful view in every direction, hardly ever a cloud, no bad winds, good water, everything healthy and clean. But let us not speak of those, which were more mansions of great lords, rather taking the form of castles than of villas. Let us not recall now the glories of the Alberti family, let us forget those proud structures with heavy ornamentation where many now pass and sigh, seeing their new inhabitants and longing for the older style of countenance and manner characteristic of our Albertis. I do say I would try to purchase a property such as my uncle Caroccio, the grandson of Messer Iacobo, knight, whose son was the second Caroccio Alberti, used to describe as ideal: a place to which one could bring a quarter peck of salt and it would be enough to feed the family all year.

This is what I would do, then. I would see that the estate was, first of all, suited to yield all that might be needed to feed the family, and if not all, at least the most necessary commodities, namely bread and wine, should both be there. As for the road to go to the estate or close to it, I would use the meadows, so that as I passed to and from the place I could look it over and see what was wanted. I could always make use of a path through it to check over the fields and the whole estate. I would also very much prefer to have the whole place united or to have the parts close together, so that I could often pass through all of it without going too much out of my way.

Lionardo: A good idea, for when you watch over workers in one place, those in another are often apt to be neglecting their work even more.

Giannozzo: This also reduces the number of peasant families one has to deal with; it is hard to believe how much wickedness there is among the plowmen raised up among the clods. Their one purpose is to cheat you, and they never let anyone deceive them in anything. All the errors are in their favor; they try constantly and by every means to get and obtain what is part of your property. First the peasant wants you to buy him an ox, goats, a sow, a mare also, and then sheep, too. Next he asks you for loans to satisfy his creditors, to clothe his wife, to dower his daughter. Finally he asks you to reinforce his hut, to rebuild various structures and improve various parts of the housing, and still he never stops complaining. Even though he be richer than his master, he is always wailing about how poor he is. He forever needs something, and he never speaks to you but to bring you some expense or burden. If the crop is abundant, he keeps the better two thirds for himself. If through bad weather or for some other reason the land was sterile in a certain year, the peasant gives you only the damage and the loss. So does he always take for himself the most or the best of what is useful, while he throws the uncomfortable and burdensome aspects of farming entirely on his teammate.

Lionardo: Perhaps, then, it would be better to spend a little more on the market in order to supply the house rather than have to deal with such ill-disposed people.

Giannozzo: On the contrary, my dear Lionardo. It is better, far better to bear the weight of such villainous ingenuities which teach you the better to tolerate your fellow citizens who may have similar inconsiderate ways—and to teach the peasants to exercise some degree of diligence. Besides, if you don't have too great a number of peasants to deal with, their malice will not be insufferable, and if you are careful they will not be able to cheat you much. You will even take much secret delight in their little tricks and laugh heartily at them.

Lionardo: I truly admire your wisdom, Giannozzo. You know how to get some edification and pleasure even out of malicious people.

Giannozzo: But of course, my children, that's what I would do. But I would try to locate this property in a place where neither a river nor heavy rains could ruin it for me by flooding, where there were no robber bands, and where the air was very pure. I hear there are farms which are otherwise fruitful and fertile where the air is full of tiny and invisible insects; they are not felt but they pass through and fly into the lungs, where they feed by gnawing at the interior, killing animals and also many people.

Lionardo: I remember reading about that in the ancient writers.

Giannozzo: So I would try to have good air as well as good land. In good air, if the fruits do not grow in great quantity, as they certainly may, still those that do grow will be much more flavorful and much better than those grown elsewhere. Add to this that good air contributes to your health whenever you visit your estate and gives you inestimable pleasure. Also, my dear Lionardo, I would strive to have an estate in such a location that the fruits and crops could reach my house without too much difficulty, and I would be particularly delighted if the estate could be near the city, for then I could go there often, often send for things, and walk every morning among fruits and fields and fig trees. While I took walks there for my own exercise, I should also oversee the workers, and they, seeing me, would rarely behave badly and would have greater sentiments of love and reverence for myself and would work the more diligently. I think, too, that there are quite a few such places situated in good air, far from floods, close to the city, fertile in bread and wine. As to the woods, I would soon have that resource also, for I would always be planting trees on my boundaries, shading thereby my neighbor's field rather than my own.

I would try to raise every delicious and rare fruit. In this I should emulate Messer Niccolaio Alberti, a man altogether devoted to refinement of every kind, who wanted his farms to contain every fine fruit that exists in any country. And what discrimination that man had! He sent to Sicily for pines the offspring of which bear fruit before they reach their seventh year. He also wanted certain pines in his gardens which bear a split pineseed, its shell broken on one side. Also, from Apulia he imported those pines which have pine nuts with such a delicate shell that you can break it with your finger, and of these he planted a whole wood. It would be a long tale to recount all the exotic and diverse fruits that man's discrimination established in his gardens. All were arranged in rows by his own hand, so that one could see and admire them with ease.

So should I do, too: I would plant many, many trees in good order and in rows, for they are more beautiful to look at if so planted, they shade the seedlings less, they litter the field less, and the workers have less difficulty in picking the fruit. And it would give me keen pleasure to plant them, to introduce and add various sorts of fruit in one place, and to tell my friends afterward how, when, and from where I had obtained such and such fruit trees. You know, Lionardo, having my trees that I planted bear good fruit would be most useful, but even if they did not bear good fruit they would be useful, since I would cut them for firewood, prune out the older ones and the least fruitful every year, and replace them with better plants. To my mind, this would be the keenest pleasure.

Lionardo: What kind of person could fail to take pleasure in his farm? The farm is of great, honorable, and reliable value. Any other occupation is fraught with a thousand risks, carries with it a mass of suspicions and of trouble, and brings numerous losses and regrets. There is trouble in purchasing, fear in transporting, anxiety in selling, apprehension in giving credit, weariness in collecting what is due you, deceit in exchange. So in all other occupations you are beset by a multitude of worries and suffer constant anxiety. The farm alone seems reliable, generous, trustworthy and truthful. Managed with diligence and love, it never wearies of repaying you. Reward follows reward. In spring the farm gives you a multitude of delights, greenery, flowers, aromas, songs. It tries to please you, it smiles and promises you a magnificent harvest, it fills you with good hopes as well as sufficient joy in the present. Then in summer how courteously it attends on you! First one sort of fruit, then another, comes to your house—your house is never empty of some gift. Then there is autumn: now the farm gives liberal reward for your labors, shows great gratitude for your merit—gladly, copiously, and faithfully serves you! Twelvefold reward is yours—for a little sweat, many casks of wine.

Your farm replaces what is old and stale in your house with what is new and fresh and clean and good, everything with generous interest. It brings you currants and other grapes to hang and dry. To this add nuts to fill your house in winter, and fragrant and beautiful apples and pears. The farm never stops sending you periodic gifts of its later fruits. Even in winter it does not fail to be generous. It sends you wood and oil and juniper and laurel, so that when you enter your house out of snow and wind you can make a joyful and aromatic fire. And if you deign to lend it your company, the farm invites you into splendid sunlight, offers hares and bucks and deer for you to chase, lets you enjoy the sport and shake off the cold and harshness of the weather.

I shall say nothing of the chickens, kids, fresh cheeses, and other delicacies produced on the farm and preserved for you in year-round supply. It amounts to this: the farm labors that you may lack for nothing in your house, that your spirit may be free of all melancholy, that you may be nourished with what is pleasant and good. If the farm also demands some work from you, this work at least is unlike other occupations that depress and worry you. It does not exhaust your energies and make you weary but fills you with joy. It tends to the benefit of your own health as well as of the farm.

Giannozzo: What need to say it all, Lionardo? You cannot praise the farm half as much as it ought to be praised. It is excellent for our health, helps maintain us, benefits the family. Good men and prudent householders are always interested in the farm, as everyone knows, and indeed the farm is, first of all, profitable and, second, a source of both pleasure and honor. There is no need, as with other occupations, to fear deceit and fraud from debtors or suppliers. Nothing goes on under cover; it is all visible and publicly understood. You will not be cheated, nor need you call in notaries and witnesses, undertake lawsuits, or engage in other irritating and depressing intrigues most of which are not worth the convulsions of spirit involved in carrying them through to a successful conclusion.

Consider, too, that you can retire to your farm and live there at peace, nurturing your little family, dealing by yourself with your own affairs, and on a holiday talking pleasantly in the shade about oxen and wool or about vines and seeds. You can live undisturbed by rumors and tales and by the wild strife that breaks out periodically in the city. You can be free of the suspicions, fears, slanders, injuries, feuds, and other miseries which are too ugly to talk about and horrible even to remember. Among all the subjects discussed on the farm there is none which can fail to delight you. All are pleasant to talk of and are heard by willing ears. Everyone tells what he knows that is useful to agriculture. Everyone teaches and corrects you where you erred in some of your planting or in your manner of sowing. The cultivation and management of fields does not give rise to envy, hate, and malevolence.

Lionardo: In addition, you enjoy on the farm clear and happy days of clean, open air. You have a lovely view when you look at those leafy hills and verdant plains. Clear springs and streams go leaping through and losing themselves in the waving grass.

, Giannozzo: Yes, by God, a true paradise. And, what is more, you can in the enjoyment of your estate escape the violence, the riots, the storm of the city, the marketplace, and the townhall. On the farm you can hide yourself and avoid seeing all the stealing and crime, the vast numbers of depraved men who are always flitting past your eyes in the city. There they never cease to chirp in your ears, to scream and bellow in the streets hour after hour, like a dangerous and disgusting kind of beast. What a blessing to live on the farm, what an unheard of happiness.

Lionardo: Do you think one should, in fact, live in the country rather than in the midst of town?

Giannozzo: As for me, seeing that it is freer of vice, involves less cares and less expense, offers more health and more enjoyment of life, yes, indeed, my children. I do praise the country estate.

Lionardo: Are you sufficiently convinced of this to raise your children there?

Giannozzo: If my children could expect to spend their whole lives never talking to any but good persons, I would certainly want to have them grow up in the country. But the number of men who are not of the very worst sort is so small that we fathers, to protect ourselves from the wicked and their many devices, must make sure that our children know them. A man cannot distinguish who is wicked if he knows nothing of wickedness. If you have never heard the sound of the bagpipe, you cannot judge the quality of the instrument. Let us imitate those who wish to become skilled shieldsmen: first we must learn to wound so that then we may know how nimbly to avoid the pointed lance and how to protect our flank from the blade. If vices dwell among men, as they do, I can see the wisdom of raising the young where vices abound no less than men, in the city.

Lionardo: Also, Giannozzo, it is in the city one learns to be a citizen. There people acquire valuable knowledge, see many models to teach them the avoidance of evils. As they look around them they notice how handsome is honor, how lovely is fame, how divine a thing is glory. There they taste the sweets of praise, of being named and esteemed and admired. By these wondrous joys the young are awakened to the pursuit of excellence and come to devote themselves to attempting difficult things worthy of immortality. Such high advantages may not, perhaps, be found in the country amid logs and clods.

Giannozzo: I have some doubts, for all that, Lionardo, as to which is better, to bring up one's children in the country or the city. But let us assess it thus: every situation has its own natural advantages. In the city are the workshops of great dreams, for such are governments, constitutions, fame. In the country we find peace, contentment, a free way of pursuing life and health. For myself I think if I had such a farm as I was describing I should wish to stay there a good part of the year and enjoy myself while cultivating the means to feed my family abundantly and well.

Lionardo: Now would you tell us also how to dress the family, another necessary expenditure you mentioned?

Giannozzo: Among first considerations, my very first would be and always has been to keep my household well dressed, each member in accordance with his station. If I neglected to do this, my flock would give me but poor loyalty, indeed my own household would hate me. I should be generally despised, those outside my family would blame me, and I should be reputed miserly. It would be no true thrift, therefore, to dress them less than well.

Lionardo: How would you have your family dress?

Giannozzo: Well, that's the point: good clothing for civic life must be clean, suitable, and well made—that's the main thing. Joyous colors are proper to wear, whatever bright colors suit the wearer best, and good cloth is imperative. The slashed garments and laces one sees on some people have never seemed attractive to me except for clowns and buglers. On great holidays a new garment, on other days clothing that has been worn. Very old clothing is only to be worn inside the house. Your clothes should bring you respect, right, my dear Lionardo? You, too, then, should give some respect to your clothes. I have given some thought to the matter, and I think people do not generally consider it as much as they should. To generous and easy spenders it may seem unimportant if you belt your robe; but in fact belting a robe is doubly wasteful. Without a belt your dress appears fuller and more dignified; in addition, the belt, of course, makes the cloth shiny and rubs off all the nap. Soon, while your robe may still be new, the waist will already be worn out and old. Beautiful clothes, therefore, should not be belted. We want to have beautiful clothes. Since they do us honor, we too should have some consideration for them.

Lionardo: Would you dress your whole household in beautiful garments?

Giannozzo: According to what was appropriate for each one, yes.

Lionardo: And would you give clothes to those who work for you in the house as a kind of bonus?

Giannozzo: I would be generous with them, indeed, if I saw they were loyal and hard working in my service and in the service of my family.

Lionardo: And I suppose you would reward them in this way.

Giannozzo: Yes, it would be a reward, and an incentive to others as well, to try to merit as much as those good servants had received from me. There is nothing like honoring and rewarding the good members effectively and surely if you want to make the whole household temperate, well conducted, and conscientious. What is praised will soon be valued by the good, and as for the not-so-good, rewards and praises given to the good kindle in them a desire to earn the same things by similar behavior and a similar character.

Lionardo: I like what you are saying. You speak most beautifully, too. I confess that this is how things are. But how would you go about getting clothes for your family? Would you sell the fruits of your farm?

Giannozzo: If there were a sufficient surplus, why not turn it into money and spend it on whatever is needed? That's always been a good thing for the whole family, if the father sells rather than buys. As you know, however, all year the family runs into small expenses for household furnishings and all sorts of things that must be made; there are also certain major expenses, of which almost the chief is for clothing. Young people grow, there are weddings to prepare, payments on dowries to be made, and if one tried to pay for it all from one's farm surplus, I think that income would prove insufficient.

I would, therefore, exercise some civic occupation as well, something suited to myself and beneficial both to me and to my relatives. In this occupation I would be able to earn money constantly and to provide for all necessities. The surplus I would keep for times of major expenditure, perhaps to aid my country, to help my friends, to give to my kinsmen, or other things like that. These are necessities that can arise at any moment, and they are not easy to cope with. Nor are they avoidable, since duty is involved, and also since one's feelings of sympathy are aroused. These, moreover, are the very deeds that gain a man friendship, reputation, and honor. I, for one, am glad to have an occupation which keeps me busy and lets me be sure my sons are not growing up lazy or idle.

Lionardo: What occupation would you choose?

Giannozzo: As honorable an occupation as possible and, if possible, one useful to many people.

Lionardo: Would it be trade, perhaps?

Giannozzo: Yes, yet to increase my tranquillity, I would like to have something secure, something I could see improving under my hands from day to day. Perhaps I would have men working wool or silk or something similar. This kind of business is less trouble and much less nerve-racking than trade. I would gladly take on an enterprise like that, which requires many hands, for the money goes to a large number of persons. It helps many poor people.

Lionardo: An act of noblest piety, it would be, to help many people.

Giannozzo: Who would deny that? Particularly if it were carried out as I would like to see it—for I would employ workers and would not use my own labor except to oversee and regulate everyone's performance of his task. Here is what I would say to all of them: be honest, fair, and friendly with everyone who comes in, with strangers no less than with friends. Be truthful and precise at all times. Beware that no one ever, through your roughness or malice, leaves your shop feeling cheated or discontented. For, my children, it is less profit than loss, I think, to gain cash and lose good will. A seller who is well liked always has plenty of customers. A good name and the affection of one's fellow citizens are worth more than the greatest amount of money. I should command them also to sell nothing at an extra high price. Whether confronted by a creditor or a debtor, they would be told always to remember to be fair and square with everyone. They must not be proud or spiteful or negligent or quarrelsome, and above all they must be most diligent in keeping records. Thus I should hope that God would grant me prosperity, that plenty of clients would fill my shop, and that my name would be widely known. These are not things to be viewed lightly, for the favor of God and the good will of men bring ever increasing profits.

Lionardo: Yet agents, Giannozzo, are often far from zealous in their work. They rarely seek to represent your interests first and their own second.

Giannozzo: For that reason I would select with care and have good and honest employees. I would keep a close check on things, too, and go over even minor transactions. Even though I already knew the answers, I should ask questions just to appear watchful. I would not do this in such a way as to seem oversuspicious and distrustful but in a way that might influence my agents to avoid becoming careless. If it is clear to my agent that nothing remains hidden from me, he thinks it essential to be both careful and truthful. Even if he wished to be just the opposite, he could not be. My checking things over carefully would mean that errors could not escape me for long. A mistake not caught today would still come out tomorrow and be corrected in good time. If something were maliciously hidden, however, believe me, a bit of cheating soon reveals itself to a master who is always turning things over and looking through them. Messer Benedetto Alberti used to say, and he was a prudent man not in public affairs only but also in every aspect of private civic life, that it was a good sign if a merchant had ink-stained fingers.

Lionardo: I am not sure I understand.

Giannozzo: He considered it essential for a merchant or anyone who does business with a large number of persons always to write everything down, to note all transactions, and to keep a record of every item brought in or taken out. As he watches over the enterprise, he should almost always have his pen in his hand. I, for one, think this an excellent precept. If you put things off from today to tomorrow, they elude you or are forgotten, and the agent finds excuses and occasions either for dishonesty or for carelessness like his master's. Don't ever suppose that others work harder for you than you for yourself—you will only lose money in the end, or lose the agent. No question about it, my dear Lionardo, it is worse to have a bad agent than to have none. A diligent master can even improve an inferior agent, but when the man who ought to be chiefly concerned is himself negligent, even a good employee tends to deteriorate.

Lionardo: How true! Even if you are a careful master, a villainous agent may rob and cheat you with clever tricks, but if he discovers that you yourself neglect your affairs, he will do you far more damage. This, too, is something we have learned in our family by all too frequent experience. We have often had employees whose villainy did us far more harm than our own negligence. But it is hard even to dissociate oneself from a dishonest man without suffering some damage.

Giannozzo: I think of all the losses and damage I have known merchants to suffer, and I think that five out of six times the catastrophe was due to the incompetence of the man who was supposed to be responsible for management. I feel I may assert with certainty that there is nothing so apt to make employees loyal as having a hard-working master, and nothing makes them worse than the master's negligence. Laziness, negligence, not watching carefully over one's business, these are the things that injure our condition, my children, and bring us down. A man who cannot report on his own affairs except by the mouth of another is a fool. He is blind who can see only with another's eyes. One must be careful, alert, and diligent. One must check everything, and at frequent intervals. Things cannot easily go astray then, and if they do they are soon found.

Neglected tasks pile up till they cannot be finished in a day. You cannot give them, then, the attention they deserve. What you might at one time have done well and with pleasure now, under the pressure created by delay, must be done hastily. You cannot now do each of the various portions of the task as well as before, in their proper time, you certainly could have. I should, therefore, work hard at every task. In the business that mattered most to me, I should, first, exercise extreme care in choosing my agent and, second, zealously investigate all things and know the business so intimately that the agent would not grow careless. To give my employees incentive to improve, I should respect them, treat them generously, and try to make them feel an attachment both to myself and to my affairs.

Lionardo: I certainly agree that one must very carefully choose good agents, and no less carefully prevent them from turning into bad ones. One must as you say, watch them diligently so that they remain, as time goes by, still loyal and zealous in your service.

Giannozzo: This is essential, and do you know how to do it? It is necessary, first, to make wide inquiries about your future agent, to inform yourself of his background, to appraise his past conduct and carefully consider his habits and character.

Lionardo: Which do you prefer as agents, outsiders or members of the family? I have often noticed quite some controversy on this point among merchants. Some say it is easier to punish a stranger and to get your full value out of him than to manage a member of your own family. Others think that outsiders are more obedient, more submissive than relatives. Others find it undesirable that their kinsmen should do so well as to arrive in time at a high place, take authority, and eventually replace the man now in command. Thus do their opinions run.

Giannozzo: As for me, my dear Lionardo, I would not even call a man my agent, but rather my enemy, if I expected to punish him, and then I would not want him among my servants. Nor do I fully understand why I should expect strangers to give me more reverence, although it is true that from my own kinsmen I would feel it more honorable to accept good will and love than obedience and servitude. I do not think, however, that to have the loyalty and zeal of men who love me is less valuable in my business than to have the obedience of such as fear me. I also would not consider a man worthy of good fortune or deserving of authority or in any sense a man to be respected if he found it painful to see his own kinsmen enjoying honor and happiness. A man would seem an utter fool to me, indeed, if he thought he could maintain his dignity and preserve his fortunate position without the favor and aid of his family. Believe me, my children, I know a great many examples to show this, but for brevity's sake, I won't recount them now. Believe me, no one can keep good fortune for any length of time unless other men put hand and shoulder to the wheel. If a man is in disgrace with his own family, he is a fool to think he could win the favor of strangers. But to look at your question more closely, Lionardo, do you assume that your relatives are good or bad people?

Lionardo: Good ones.

Giannozzo: Well, if they are good ones, I am very sure that they will be better in my service than strangers. It seems reasonable to me, first, to assume that my own people will be more loyal and affectionate than outsiders and, second, to prefer to do them a favor rather than to help others.

Lionardo: But what if they are bad?

Giannozzo: How bad, Lionardo? If they are incompetent, Lionardo, would I not be under a greater obligation to instruct my own relatives than to do the same for strangers?

Lionardo: Yes, certainly, but what if, as sometimes does happen, they cheated?

Giannozzo: Tell me, Lionardo, would you find it more distasteful to discover that one of your own kinsmen had acquired goods of yours or that a stranger had stolen them?

Lionardo: It would trouble me less if my wealth were useful to one of my kinsmen, but I would be more indignant at the betrayal by one whom I had trusted more.

Giannozzo: Erase that false opinion from your mind, Lionardo. Don't believe that a kinsman would ever cheat you if you treated him like a kinsman. What relative of yours would not rather deal with you than with a stranger? A stranger, indeed, only joins you to gain what he can for himself.

Remember this—I keep repeating it because it is something you should always keep in mind—there is more honor and value in helping your own family than outsiders. The little or much that the stranger takes away with him will never come back into the possession of your family, nor will it be useful in any way to your grandchildren. If a stranger grows rich with you, he will have small gratitude toward you, because, as he thinks, he has earned it. Your own kinsman, benefiting by association with you, will admit his obligation and will retain a memory that makes him eager to help your own children in a similar way. Even should he fail to be grateful and to recognize your benificence, if you are good and just you would sooner see your own kinsman enjoy prosperity than any outsider whatsoever. This is something you need never fear anyway, as you should realize, if only you are diligent in making a careful choice of agent and watchful to keep him from slipping.

Tell me something else, however—when you are choosing an agent, in which case will you find it more difficult to learn what his true character is, if you take him from your own family, who grew up under your eyes and with whom you have conversed every day, or if you draw him from among strangers, whom you know much less well and have far less experience of? I believe, Lionardo, that it is far more difficult to know the mind of a stranger than to know one of your own relatives. If so, and if to make a good choice we need to know and to investigate character, who would ever think it easier to accomplish that task with a stranger? Who could prefer a stranger whom he did not know well to one of his own family whom he did know well?

When our relatives are good and talented, we should help them, and when they are not already endowed with these qualities, we should apply all our efforts and give them all our help, to make them gradually improve. It is a sign of meager charity if a man disdains his own people to benefit others. It is a sign of grave disloyalty to distrust one's own kin while trusting other men. But perhaps I go on too long on this point. What do you think about it Lionardo?

Lionardo: Your opinion seems to me charitable, just, and true. It is my own belief, too, and perhaps, if everyone held it as tenaciously as I, our family would not now have so much cause to complain of injuries sometimes received from strangers. Certainly I admit the wisdom of your view; I might put it this way—the man who does not love his family does not know how to love.

Giannozzo: How true that is. If you can have the service of your kinsmen, never, never call on others. And it is a good thing if you solicit their service, take pleasure in teaching them, enjoy being accounted a father to them. You can give yourself the happiness of having a great number of young people who, thanks to your kindness, stand to you as children. In aspiration and action, they will always live in harmony with you. The stranger does not do all this. Instead, as soon as he has begun to know a little something or to gather a little property, he wants to be a partner. Soon he tells you he wants to leave, creates difficulties in order to force you to improve his condition. He cares little whether you suffer harm or disgrace as long as he profits. But let that go.

I could bring forward an infinite number of arguments to show that a stranger abides with you as an enemy, while a kinsman is always your friend. Relatives seek your welfare and your good name. They want to avoid any harm befalling you or any disgrace coming to you, for every honor that you gain brings them honor also, and part of the dishonor attached to any disgrace of yours falls on them. A crowd of further reasons rushes to mind by which I might clearly show you that it is better form, more honorable, more practical, more noble, and safer to draw your help from your family, not from outside. Even if you should think the opposite, I counsel you always to show greater charity toward your own kin than toward strangers. I would remind you how great is our debt toward the young, how much it is our duty to teach them excellence and to guide them toward honor. To us, fathers of families, surely it is a terrible disgrace if we hold back available honor and benefit from our own family, as if we disdained and despised them.

Lionardo: I don't need to hear any more reasons. I consider it a real disgrace if a man will not answer the needs of his own relatives. I also admit that one who cannot live on good terms with his own kind will be still less able to live happily with outsiders.

These young people and I are deeply obliged to you for your remarks, for they are of the most extraordinary value for good household management. It would be a still greater gift and paternal kindness if you would let us hear the rest also. We do know that more should follow. You have spoken of the house, of the farm, and of the occupation which good management requires. Teach us now how to deal with the further expenditures which arise every day, besides those for clothing, food, and the liberal entertainment of friends. There are times when we ought to undertake some expense for the honor and fame of our house. On a number of occasions our family has embarked on such expenditures, among them the construction added by our fathers to the temple of the Agnoli, and to many other places within and outside our city. They built at San Miniato, at Paradiso, at Santa Caterina, and added to various other public and private edifices like these. Now what rule or method would you say applied to this kind of spending? I know that for this, as for the other sort, you can probably give us some excellent principles.

Giannozzo: None better than some I know.

Lionardo: And what are they?

Giannozzo: Listen. I have certain ideas about this—now you think, too, and see if I am right. It seems to me, you see, that all expenses are either necessary or unnecessary. I call those expenses necessary without which the family cannot be honorably maintained. The man who fails to spend for these purposes harms his own honor and the comfort of his family. The greater the harm it does not to make a certain purchase, the more necessary is that purchase. The number of such expenses is so great it would be hard to count them all, but they may be summed up in the fact that together they comprise the whole acquisition and maintenance of the house, the farm, and the shop. These in turn are the three sources of all that is useful and valuable and needed by the family. Unnecessary expenses, on the other hand, are those which give pleasure if undertaken wisely, but which it does no harm to omit. Among these are works like the frescoes for the loggia, the silver, embellishments that add pomp to one's way of life, like fine clothing and largesse. Likewise unnecessary but not unreasonable are the expenses which one undertakes in pursuit of pleasure and civilized distraction, expenditures without which you could still live honorably and well.

Lionardo: I understand: like buying beautiful books, handsome steeds, and other things that attract a proud and liberal spirit.

Giannozzo: Exactly.

Lionardo: These might be called voluntary expenditures, then, since they satisfy our will rather than our necessity.

Giannozzo: All right. Beyond these there are also insane expenditures, the ones that bring disgrace on the man who plunges into them. Such would be the cost of keeping serpents in one's house, or other still more terrible, cruel, and poisonous beasts than these.

Lionardo: Tigers maybe?

Giannozzo: Worse than tigers, my dear Lionardo, nurturing wicked and depraved persons. Wicked men are worse than tigers or any beasts however dangerous. A single member of the family thus devoted to evil can ruin them all. There is no worse poison, nothing as unhealthy as the words of a wicked tongue. No madness compares with the madness driving the spiteful talker. And if a man supports such criminals as these, he certainly engages in expenses that are mad and bestial, and earns justified contempt. One should avoid acquaintance or intimacy with evil speakers like the plague. These talkers and scoundrels come between a family and its friends and acquaintances. One should never cultivate the friendship of men who willingly consort with such scoundrels. If a man loves dissipated men, he loves dissipation; and if he loves dissipation he is not good; and good men have never cared to befriend the wicked. It is neither useful nor easy, in any case, to gain the friendship of men whose doors and ears are not securely locked against malicious tongues.

Lionardo: Giannozzo, you are surely telling us the truth. These expenses are not only mad, but dangerous. Malicious people with their spitefulness usually, by means of gossip and false accusations, even manage to make you feel suspicion and hate of your own family. You will then not even believe those who truly love you and try to warn you of the wicked spite that animates those persons.

Giannozzo: Let us never take on these mad expenses, or anything of the kind. These are ways to be shunned. If anyone invites or even counsels you to act this way, he is not a man to heed or trust.

Lionardo: And by what method, Giannozzo, are we to manage the other two kinds of expenses, the necessary and the voluntary?

Giannozzo: What do you think? Do you know what my system is with necessary expenditures? I get them out of the way as fast as I can.

Lionardo: Don't you deliberate first about the best way of handling them?

Giannozzo: Yes, certainly. Don't imagine that I ever rush madly into anything if I can help it. I try to do these things with deliberate speed.

Lionardo: Why?

Giannozzo: Because if something must be done I like to get it done quickly, if only to have it off my mind. I pay what I must pay immediately. Voluntary expenses I handle quite differently, for a good reason.

Lionardo: What is your way?

Giannozzo: It's the best and most sensible method. I'll tell you I go slow, Lionardo, I delay again and again. I go as slow as I can.

Lionardo: And why?

Giannozzo: For a very good reason.

Lionardo: I want to know what good reason moves you, for I know you do nothing without the best of reasons.

Giannozzo: I'll tell you, to see if this particular desire will leave me along the way. If not, then to give myself time to think how I may fulfill it with a minimum of expense and with most satisfaction.

Lionardo: I thank you, Giannozzo. You have now taught me the way to avoid many expenses which I, like other young men, have hardly been able to avoid.

Giannozzo: That is the reason why reverence toward us elders is a duty. Thus you young men profit by asking your elders about your problems and hearing their advice. Many things in this world are better understood by experience than by speculation and theory. We who are not schooled in books become erudite through practice and time. We have considered the whole art of living and sorted out what it is best to do. We undoubtedly know, by virtue of experience, more than you with all your learning and subtleties and wily schemes. I'll tell you this, too, the shortest way to what you call good philosophy, as I've always thought, is to frequent and treasure the conversation of your elders. Ask them questions, listen to them, and obey their injunctions. Time, the best teacher of all things, has instructed the old and taught them to do those things that help us mortals get along in life and reach at last the haven of a quiet, tranquil, and respected old age.

Lionardo: We certainly expected to learn many valuable things from you, but with this, as with many of your other remarkable and precious remarks, you have far surpassed our expectations. You have taught us more than I ever thought was connected with the good management of the household. But I wonder if I am right about something. It is my impression, Giannozzo, that to undertake to be the father of a family as you have defined him to us would be a heavy task: managing one's own possessions, ruling and moderating the affections of the spirit, curbing and restraining the appetites of the body, adapting oneself and making good use of time, watching over and governing the family, preserving one's property, maintaining the house, cultivating the farm, managing the shop—all these are things which it would not be easy to do really well even if one undertook only one or another of them. To combine them all and, difficult as they are, to give each no less attention than it requires would be well nigh impossible.

Giannozzo: Don't take that attitude—these things are not what they may seem to you now, my dear Lionardo, they are not as difficult as you think now. They are all so closely connected and intertwined that, if a man tries to be a good father to his family and takes good care of one of his duties, the others follow by themselves. If a man knows how to keep from wasting time, he knows almost everything. If he knows how to make good use of time, he can be lord of anything he pleases. Even if these were hard duties, however, they offer so much practical advantage and pleasure to those who are devoted, and lay so heavy a burden of disgrace on anyone who is negligent that your interest should never cool or weary. To any good person not subject to laziness and apathy, they should be a delight. It should give us pleasure to concern ourselves with these things. Nothing is so pleasant as to satisfy ourselves, nothing gives so much satisfaction as doing what we like. We should view it as a point of honor, also, to take proper care of our own affairs, since we know by experience that neglecting them brings no less disgrace than disadvantage.

Should you still be anxious to lighten your burden, then undertake to do only part of all your work yourself, the part which best suits your mind, age, temperament, and position. Always keep your authority over all of it, however, so that your concerns are as honorably handled as they should be. You must not submit them completely to the hands and judgment of others, but only let others, as your servants, act according to your own will and plan. You must, therefore, take the responsibility for the good of all your people. Keep your agents distributed over your various affairs, one on the farm, one in the city, others where needed, and everyone doing the job that best suits his abilities.

You, men of letters, when you discuss practical wisdom and life in general, often draw a parallel with the life of ants, and say that we should learn from them to be providential and to think of the future. Messer Benedetto Alberti, I remember, often followed that literary example. He was a man who studied and who zealously applied himself to books while at home. Outside his home, he was a gregarious person. He was always discussing with attentive fellow citizens and friends matters both honorable and beautiful, both pleasant and useful, applying a characteristic mixture of wit and gravity. On the same principle, you often draw an illustration from the bees, who unite in obedience to a single leader and are all busy for the sake of the general good. They work with manly vigor and passionate zeal, some reaping precious pollen from the flowers, others bearing the burden home, some distributing it among the workers, others building the house. All together defend the riches and delights they have accumulated. You have many such analogies by means of which to make your point and to delight your hearers. Let me now also draw an analogy, if not so perfectly appropriate as yours, still not wholly misplaced. I may thus be able to set what I think more perfectly and more clearly before you. I shall almost paint it for you, placing before your very eyes the idea of what a father should do. Allow me, therefore, now to follow you in this respected and noble custom.

You know the spider and how he constructs his web. All the threads spread out in rays, each of which, however long, has its source, its roots or birthplace, as we might say, at the center. From there each filament starts and moves outward. The most industrious creature himself then sits at that spot and has his residence there. He remains in that place once his work is spun and arranged, but keeps so alert and watchful that if there is a touch on the finest and most distant thread he feels it instantly, instantly appears, and instantly takes care of the situation. Let the father of a family do likewise. Let him arrange his affairs and place them so that all look up to him alone as head, so that all are directed by him and by him attached to secure foundations. The father of the family should reside, then, in the midst of all, alert and quick to feel and to see everything, ready, wherever there is need of intervention, to provide it immediately. I don't know, Lionardo, how little this analogy of mine may suit you.

Lionardo: How could I find fault with anything you say? I swear to you, Giannozzo, I have never seen so apt or so useful an analogy. I certainly understand; it is indeed as you say. The system and diligence of the master makes even the heaviest and most difficult tasks easy and manageable. For some reason, however, I don't know why, it still does seem that public affairs get in the way of private ones, while private needs often conflict with our attention to public affairs. I am led to doubt, therefore, that all our devotion, given to all things at once, will prove sufficient.

Giannozzo: Don't take that view when there is a quick and excellent remedy at hand.

Lionardo: What remedy?

Giannozzo: Let the father of the family follow my example. Since I find it no easy matter to deal with the needs of the household when I must often be engaged outside with other men in arranging matters of wider consequence, I have found it wise to set aside a certain amount for outside use, for investments and purchases. The rest, which takes care of all the smaller household affairs, I leave to my wife's care. I have done it this way, for, to tell the truth, it would hardly win us respect if our wife busied herself among the men in the marketplace, out in the public eye. It also seems somewhat demeaning to me to remain shut up in the house among women when I have manly things to do among men, fellow citizens and worthy and distinguished foreigners.

I don't know whether you will approve of my solution. I know some people are always checking on their own household and rummaging around in every nook and cranny lest something remain hidden from them. Nothing is so obscure that they do not look into it and poke their fingers in. They say that it is no shame or harm to a man to attend carefully to his own affairs and to lay down the law and custom in his own house. They point out that Niccolo Alberti, who was a very diligent person, said diligence and universal vigilance was the mother of wealth. I too admire and like this saying, for diligence always helps; but I cannot convince myself that men who are engaged in other concerns really ought to be or to seem so very interested in every little household trifle. I don't know, perhaps I am wrong about this. What do you say, Lionardo, what do you think?

Lionardo: I agree, for you are, indeed, precisely of the opinion of the ancients. They used to say that men are by nature of a more elevated mind than women. They are more suited to struggle with arms and with cunning against the misfortunes which afflict country, religion, and one's own children. The character of men is stronger than that of women and can bear the attacks of enemies better, can stand strain longer, is more constant under stress. Therefore men have the freedom to travel with honor in foreign lands, acquiring and gathering the goods of fortune. Women, on the other hand, are almost all timid by nature, soft, slow, and therefore more useful when they sit still and watch over our things. It is as though nature thus provided for our well-being, arranging for men to bring things home and for women to guard them. The woman, as she remains locked up at home, should watch over things by staying at her post, by diligent care and watchfulness. The man should guard the woman, the house, and his family and country, but not by sitting still. He should exercise his spirit and his hands in brave enterprise, even at the cost of sweat and blood. No doubt of it, therefore, Giannozzo, those idle creatures who stay all day among the little females or who keep their minds occupied with little feminine trifles certainly lack a masculine and glorious spirit. They are contemptible in their apparent inclination to play the part of women rather than that of men. A man demonstrates his love of high achievements by the pride he takes in his own. But if he does not shun trifling occupations, clearly he does not mind being regarded as effeminate. It seems to me, then, that you are entirely right to leave the care of minor matters to your wife and to take upon yourself, as I have always seen you do, all manly and honorable concerns.

Giannozzo: Yes, you see that's my long-standing conviction. I believe that a man who is the father of a family not only should do all that is proper to a man, but that he must abstain from such activities as properly pertain to women. The details of housekeeping he should commit entirely into their hands. I always do.

Lionardo: You, however, can congratulate yourself on having a wife who probably surpasses other women. I don't know how many women one could find as vigorous and as wise in their rule of the household as your wife.

Giannozzo: My wife certainly did turn into a perfect mother for my household. Partly this was the result of her particular nature and temperament, but mainly it was due to my instruction.

Lionardo: Then you taught her?

Giannozzo: Many things.

Lionardo: And how did you do it?

Giannozzo: Well, I'll tell you. After my wife had been settled in my house a few days, and after her first pangs of longing for her mother and family had begun to fade, I took her by the hand and showed her around the whole house. I explained that the loft was the place for grain and that the stores of wine and wood were kept in the cellar. I showed her where things needed for the table were kept, and so on, through the whole house. At the end there were no household goods of which my wife had not learned both the place and the purpose. Then we returned to my room, and, having locked the door, I showed her my treasures, silver, tapestry, garments, jewels, and where each thing had its place.

Lionardo: All those valuables, then, were assigned some place in your room, I suppose because they were safer there, better secluded and more securely locked up.

Giannozzo: Yes, but primarily so that I could look them over whenever I liked without witnesses. You may be sure, children, that it is imprudent to live so openly that the whole household knows everything. It is less difficult to guard a thing from a few persons than from all. If something is known only to a few, it is easier to keep safe. If it does get lost, it is easier to get it back from a few than from many. For this and for many other reasons, I have always thought it a good precaution to keep every precious thing I had well hidden if possible, and locked up out of the reach of most hands and eyes. These treasures, I always felt, should be kept where they are safe from fire and other disaster, and where I can frequently, whether for my pleasure or to check them over, shut myself up′ alone or with whomever I choose while giving no cause for undue curiosity to those outside. No place seemed more suited for this purpose than the room where I slept. There, as I was saying, I wanted none of my precious things to be hidden from my wife. I opened to her all my household treasures, unfolded them, and showed them to her. .

Only my books and records and those of my ancestors did I determine to keep well sealed both then and thereafter. These my wife not only could not read, she could not even lay hands on them. I kept my records at all times not in the sleeves of my dress, but locked up and arranged in order in my study, almost like sacred and religious objects. I never gave my wife permission to enter that place, with me or alone. I also ordered her, if she ever came across any writing of mine, to give it over to my keeping at once. To take away any taste she might have for looking at my notes or prying into my private affairs, I often used to express my disapproval of bold and forward females who try too hard to know about things outside the house and about the concerns of their husband and of men in general. I used to remind her of a truth which Messer Cipriano Alberti once voiced to me. A most honest and wise man, Messer Cipriano once saw that the wife of a good friend of his was overeager to ask and inquire into the place where her husband had stayed the night and the company he had kept. He was anxious to warn her as best he could and to show her the respect he perhaps felt he owed to his friend. Finally he said to her, "I counsel you, friend, for your own good—be far more eager to learn what goes on in your own house than to find out about what lies outside it. Let me remind you as I would a sister that wise men say a woman who spies too much on men may be suspected of having men too much on her mind, being perhaps secretly anxious whether others are learning about her own character when she appears too interested in them. Think for yourself whether either of these passions is becoming to a lady of unblemished honor." Thus Messer Cipriano, and thus I too, spoke to my wife.

I always tried to make sure, first that she could not, and second that she did not wish, to know more of my secrets than I cared to impart. One should never, in fact, tell a secret, even a trivial one, to one's wife or any woman. I am greatly displeased with those husbands who take counsel with their wives and don't know how to confine any kind of secret to their own breast. They are madmen if they think true prudence or good counsel lies in the female brain, and still more clearly mad if they suppose that a wife will be more constant in silence concerning her husband's business than he himself has proved. Stupid husbands to blab to their wives and forget that women themselves can do anything sooner than keep quiet! For this very reason I have always tried carefully not to let any secret of mine be known to a woman. I did not doubt that my wife was most loving, and more discreet and modest in her ways than any, but I still considered it safer to have her unable, and not merely unwilling, to harm me.

Lionardo: An excellent lesson. You have been no less wise than fortunate if your wife has never dragged any secret out of you.

Giannozzo: Never, my dear Lionardo, and I'll tell you why. First, she was very modest and never cared to know more than was her business. Furthermore, I made it a rule never to speak with her of anything but household matters or questions of conduct, or of the children. Of these matters I spoke a good deal to her. From what I said, and by answering me and discussing with me, she learned the principles she required and how to apply them. I did this, also, my dear Lionardo, in order to make it impossible for her to enter into discussions with me concerning my more important and private affairs. This was my practice: I always kept my secrets and my notes carefully hidden; everything else of a domestic nature, I thought then and later, could properly be delegated to her. I did not, however, leave things so much in her hands as to be uninterested or not examine the details and be sure all was well managed.

When my wife had seen and understood the place of everything in the house, I said to her, "My dear wife, those things are to be as useful and precious to you as to me. The loss of them would injure and grieve you, therefore should you guard them no less zealously than I do. You have seen our treasures now, and thanks be to God they are such that we ought to be contented with them. If we know how to preserve them, these things will serve you and me and our children. It is up to you, therefore, my dear wife, to keep no less careful watch over them than I."

Lionardo: And what did your wife say to that?

Giannozzo: She replied by saying that her father and mother had taught her to obey them and had ordered her always to obey me, and so she was prepared to do anything I told her to. "My dear wife," said I, "a girl who knows how to obey her father and mother soon learns to please her husband. But do you know how we shall try to be? We shall imitate those who stand guard on the walls of the city; if one of them, by chance, falls asleep, he does not take it amiss for his companion to wake him up that he may do his duty for his country. Likewise, my dear wife, if you ever see any fault in me, I shall be very grateful to you for letting me know. In that way I shall know that our honor and our welfare and the good of our children are dear to your heart. Likewise be not displeased if I awaken you where there is need. Where I am lacking, you shall make it good, and so together we shall try to surpass each other in love and in zeal.

This property, this family, and the children to be born to us will belong to us both, to you as much as to me, to me as much as to you. It behooves us, therefore, not to think how much each of us has brought into our marriage, but how we can best maintain all that belongs to both of us. I shall try to obtain outside what you need inside the house; you must see that none of it is wasted.

Lionardo: How did she seem to take all this? Was she pleased?

Giannozzo: Very much so. She said she would be happy to do conscientiously whatever she knew how to do and had the skill to do, hoping it might please me. To this I said, "Dear wife, listen to me. I shall be most pleased if you do just three things: first, my wife, see that you never want another man to share this bed but me. You understand." She blushed and cast down her eyes. Still I repeated that she should never receive anyone into that room but myself. That was the first point. The second, I said, was that she should take care of the household, preside over it with modesty, serenity, tranquillity, and peace. That was the second point. The third thing, I said, was that she should see that nothing went wrong in the house.

Lionardo: Did you show her how to do what you commanded, or did she already have an expert knowledge of these things?

Giannozzo: Do not imagine, my dear Lionardo, that a young girl can ever be very well versed in these matters. Nor is such cleverness and cunning required from a young girl as it is from the mother of a family. Her modesty and virtue, on the other hand, must be much greater. And these very qualities my wife had in abundance. In these virtues she surpassed all other women. I could not describe to you how reverently she replied to me. She said her mother had taught her only how to spin and sew, and how to be virtuous and obedient. Now she would gladly learn from me how to rule the family and whatever I might wish to teach her.

Lionardo: And you, Giannozzo, how did you manage to teach her these things?

Giannozzo: What things? How to sleep with no other man but myself, perhaps?

Lionardo: You are wonderful, Giannozzo. Even in giving us these holy and austere lessons, you know how to joke and make us laugh.

Giannozzo: It certainly would be funny if I had tried to teach her how to sleep alone. I don't know if those ancient authors you like to read were able to teach that.

Lionardo: Everything but that. They do say, however, how they instructed their wives never, in bearing and behavior, to let themselves appear less virtuous than they really were. It is also described how they tried to persuade women, for this very reason, never to paint their faces with white powder, brazilnut dye, or other make-up.

Giannozzo: I myself, I assure you, did not omit this.

Lionardo: I would like to hear how you handled it. When I have a wife of my own I should like to know how to do something which, it seems, few husbands can manage. For everyone hates to see make-up on his wife, yet no one seems able to prevent it.

Giannozzo: In dealing with this problem, I exercised great discretion. You'll not be sorry to hear my fine method for making her detest the stuff. So, since it will be most useful to you to have heard me, listen carefully now. When I had given the house over to my wife's keeping, I brought her back to our own locked room, as I was saying. Then she and I knelt down and prayed to God to give us the power to make good use of those possessions which he, in his mercy and kindness, had allowed us to enjoy. We also prayed with most devoted mind that he might grant us the grace to live together in peace and harmony for many happy years, and with many male children, and that he might grant to me riches, friendship, and honor, and to her, integrity, purity, and the character of a perfect mistress of the household. Then, when we had stood up, I said to her:

"My dear wife, to have prayed God for these things is not enough. Let us also be very diligent and conscientious and do our best to obtain what we have prayed for. I, my dear wife, shall seek with all my powers to gain what we have asked of God. You, too, must set your whole will, all your mind, and all your modesty to work to make yourself a person whom God has heard and to whom he has granted what you prayed for. You should realize that in this regard nothing is so important for yourself, so acceptable to God, so pleasing to me, and precious in the sight of your children as your chastity. The woman's character is the jewel of her family; the mother's purity has always been a part of the dowry she passes on to her daughters; her purity has always far outweighed her beauty. A beautiful face is praised, but unchaste eyes make it ugly through men's scorn, and too often flushed with shame or pale with sorrow and melancholy. A handsome person is pleasing to see, but a shameless gesture or an act of incontinence in an instant renders her appearance vile. Unchastity angers God, and you know that God punishes nothing so severely in women as he does this lack. All their lives he makes them notorious and miserable. The shameless woman is hated by her whose love is true and good. She soon discovers that, in fact, her dishonored condition pleases only her enemies. Only one who wishes us to suffer and be troubled can rejoice when he sees you fall from honor.

"Shun every sort of dishonor, my dear wife. Use every means to appear to all people as a highly respectable woman. To seem less would be to offend God, me, our children, and yourself. To seem so, indeed, brings praise and love and favor from all. Then you can hope that God will give some aid to your prayers and vows.

"To be praised for your chastity, you must shun every deed that lacks true nobility, eschew any sort of improper speech, avoid giving any sign that your spirit lacks perfect balance and chastity. You will disdain, first of all, those vanities which some females imagine will please men. All made up and plastered and painted and dressed in lascivious and im-proper clothing, they suppose they are more attractive to men than when adorned with pure simplicity and true virtue. Vain and foolish women are these who imagine that when they appear in make-up and look far from virtuous they will be praised by those who see them. They do not realize that they are provoking disapproval and harming themselves. Nor do they realize, in their petty vanity, that their immodest appearance excites numerous lustful men. Such men all besiege and attack such a girl, some with suddenness, some with persistence, some with trickery, until at last the unfortunate wretch falls into real disgrace. From such a fall she cannot rise again without the stain of great and lasting infamy upon her."

Thus I spoke to my wife. To convince her still more fully of the danger, as well as of the shame, in a woman's covering her face with the powders and poisons which the silly creatures call make-up, see, dear Lionardo, what a nice lesson I gave her. There was a saint in the room, a very lovely statue of silver, whose head and hands alone were of purest ivory. It was set, polished and shining, in the center of the altar, as usual. "My dear wife," I said to her, "suppose you besmirched the face of this image in the morning with chalk and calcium and other ointments. It might well gain in color and whiteness. In the course of the day the wind would carry dust to it and make it dirty, but in the evening you would wash it, and then, the next day, cover it again with ointments, and then wash it again. Tell me, after many days of this, if you wanted to sell it, all polished and painted, how much money do you think you would get for it? More than if you had never begun painting it?

"Much less," she replied.

"That's right," said I, "for the buyer of the image does not buy it for a coating of paint which can be put on or off but because he appreciates the excellence of the statue and the skill of the artist. You would have lost your labor, then, as well as the cost of those ointments. Tell me, though, if you went on for months or years washing and redaubing it, would you make it more beautiful?"

"I think not," she said.

"On the contrary, you would spoil it and wear it out. You would scrape off the finish of the ivory. It would become rough and end up colorless, yellowed, softened by those powders. Certainly. But if those poultices could have that effect on ivory, which is hard stuff by nature and able to last forever if left alone, you can be sure, my dear wife, that they can do your own brow and cheeks still greater harm. For your skin is tender and delicate if you don't smear anything on it, and if you do it will soon grow rough and flabby. Don't deny that those things are poison. You know that all those make-up materials do contain poison. They do you much more harm than they would to ivory. You know, even the least bit of dust or a drop of sweat makes a smear on your face. No, you will not be more beautiful with that stuff, only dirty, and in the long run you will ruin your skin."

Lionardo: Did she seem to agree and to realize you were telling the truth?

Giannozzo: What sort of silly girl would fail to realize this was the truth? Besides, to make sure she did believe me, I asked her about a neighbor of mine, a woman who had few teeth left in her mouth, and those appeared tarnished with rust. Her eyes were sunken and always inflamed, the rest of her face whithered and ashen. All her flesh looked decomposed and disgusting. Her silvery hair was the only thing about her that one might regard without displeasure. So I asked my wife whether she wished she were blond and looked like her?

"Heavens, no," said she.

"And why not? Does she seem so old to you? How old do you think she is?"

To that she replied most modestly that she was no judge of these matters, but to her the woman seemed about the age of her mother's wetnurse. Then I assured her of the truth, namely that that neighbor of mine was born less than two years before me and had certainly not yet attained her thirty-second year. Thanks to make-up, however, she had been left in this diseased condition and seemed old before her time.

When I saw she was really amazed at this, I reminded her of all the Alberti girls, of my cousins and others in the family. "You see, my dear wife," I said, "how fresh and lively our girls all are, for the simple reason that they never anoint themselves with anything but river water. And so shall you do, my wife," said I. "You'll not poison yourself or whiten your face to make yourself seem more beautiful for me. You are white and bright enough complexioned for me as you are. Rather, like the Alberti girls, you will just wash and keep clean with water alone. My dear wife, there is no one but me for you to think of pleasing in this matter. Me, however, you cannot please by deception. Remember that. You cannot deceive me, anyway, because I see you at all hours and know very well how you look without make-up. As for outsiders, if you love me, think how could any of them matter more to you than your own husband. Remember, my dear wife, that a girl who tries harder to please outsiders than the one she should be pleasing shows that she loves her husband less than she does strangers."

Lionardo: Wise words. But did she obey you?

Giannozzo: It is true that at weddings, sometimes, whether because she was embarrassed at being among so many people or heated with dancing, she sometimes appeared to have more than her normal color. In the house, however, there was only one time, when friends and their wives were invited to dinner at Easter. My wife, on this occasion, had covered her face with pumice, in God's name, and she talked all too animatedly with each guest on his arrival or departure. She was showing off and being merry with everyone, as I observed.

Lionardo: Did you get angry with her?

Giannozzo: Ah, Lionardo, I never got angry with my wife.

Lionardo: Never?

Giannozzo: Why should we let quarrels arise between ourselves? Neither of us ever desired from the other anything that was not wholly right.

Lionardo: Yet I imagine you must have been troubled if in this matter your wife failed to obey you as she should have.

Giannozzo: Yes, yes, true enough. But I did not, for all that, show her that I was troubled.

Lionardo: Didn't you scold her?

Giannozzo: Ha, ha, yes, in the right way. To me it has always seemed obvious, dear children, that the way to correct someone is to begin gently, put out the evil quickly, and kindle good will. This you can learn from me—it is much better to reprimand a woman temperately and gently than with any sort of harsh severity. A slave can bear threats and blows and perhaps not grow indignant if you shout at him. A wife, however, will obey you better from love than from fear. Any free spirit will sooner set out to please you than to submit to you. It is best, therefore, to do as I did and correct your wife's failing kindly but in time.

Lionardo: How did you reprimand her?

Giannozzo: I waited till we were alone. Then I smiled at her and said, "Oh dear, how did your face get dirty? Did you by any chance bump into a pan? Go wash yourself, quick, before these people begin to make fun of you. The lady and mother of a household must always be neat and clean if she wants the rest of the family to learn good conduct and modest demeanor."

She understood me and at once began to cry. I let her go wash off both tears and make-up. After that I never had to tell her again.

Lionardo: What a perfect wife. I can well believe that such a woman, so obedient to your word and so modest by her own nature, could elicit respect and good behavior in the rest of the household.

Giannozzo: All wives are thus obedient, if their husbands know how to be husbands. But some I see quite unwisely suppose that they can win obedience and respect from a wife to whom they openly and abjectly subject themselves. If they show by word and gesture that their spirit is all too deeply lascivious and feminine, they certainly make their wives no less unfaithful than rebellious. Never, at any moment, did I choose to show in word or action even the least bit of self-surrender in front of my wife. I did not imagine for a moment that I could hope to win obedience from one to whom I had confessed myself a slave. Always, therefore, I showed myself virile and a real man. Always I encouraged her to love virtue. Always I reminded her to be most disciplined. I kept her always conscious of all that I, myself, knew was right for a perfect mother of a family and wanted her to know also.

"My dear wife," I often told her, "if we want to live in peace and harmony, all our household must be well behaved and modest in their ways. You must gladly take on yourself the task of making them obedient and respectful toward yourself. Unless you yourself are very modest and self-restrained, however, you may be sure that what you cannot do for yourself you can still less produce in others. To be regarded as a very modest and restrained woman, you must be such that all vileness offends you. This will help to discipline the household, for all its members will take care not to displease you. Unless they have the highest example of chastity and decorum in you, however, do not expect them to show obedience, let alone reverence, toward yourself. Respect is something one must earn. Only character gives a man dignity, and one who wears dignity can gain respect; one who can gain respect can win obedience. One who does not live up to his own standards soon loses all dignity and all respect. Therefore, dear wife, make it your concern to be and to appear in every gesture, word, and deed most modest and most virtuous.

"A great part of modesty, remember, consists in tempering all one's gestures with gravity and a mature manner. One must temper one's mind and every word of one's speech, even within the household and among one's own family, all the more outside among strangers. I shall be truly glad if I see that you disdain the frivolous mannerisms, the habit of tossing the hands about, the chattering that some little girls do all day, in the house, at the door, and wherever they go. They talk now with this friend, now with that one; they ask a lot of questions and say a lot of things that they don't know as well as a lot that they do. All that is the way to get yourself the reputation of an irresponsible featherbrain. Silence is as it always has been, the peak of dignity and the source of respect for a woman. Talking too much has been ever the habit and sign of a silly fool. So be glad to listen quietly and to talk less than you listen. If you do talk, never on any account tell our secrets to others or be too eager to know their affairs. A woman who spends all day chattering and agitating about things that do not concern the welfare of her household, while neglecting the things that do, indulges an ugly habit and brings contempt on herself. But if you govern the family with proper diligence, you will preserve and put to good use all the resources of the household."

Lionardo: And I imagine you taught her the management of the household as you taught her other things?

Giannozzo: Don't you doubt it. Of course I did my best to make her in every way an excellent mother of the household. "Dear wife," I told her, "you should view it as your job to give the house such an orderly routine that no one is ever idle. Give everyone some suitable job to do. And where you see reliable loyalty and hard work, give all the responsibility that may properly be given. At the same time, keep your eye on what everyone is doing. Make sure that those who are busy with things that are useful and beneficial for the family are aware that you will witness their merit. If someone works more diligently and lovingly at his task than the others, be sure, dear wife, that you do not forget to praise him in their presence. Thus in the future he will long to be still more helpful every day, knowing he can count on your appreciation. The others will want to please you, too, as much as those you have praised most. Together, let us reward everyone according to his merit. In that way we shall make all our servants loyal and devoted to us and our affairs."

Lionardo: But, Giannozzo, we all know that servants and even other members of the household are apt to be persons of small intelligence. Generally if they had more capacity for work and finer feelings, they would not stay with us but would learn some other trade. Did you teach your wife how to handle rough and uncouth persons, therefore, and how to make them obey her?

Giannozzo: The fact is that servants are as obedient as masters are skilled in commanding. Some people as I have observed myself, want their servants to obey them in matters where they themselves can give no direction. Others never know how to be the real master or to convince others that that's what they are. Remember, my children, no servant will listen and obey unless you know how to command. Nor will any resist and rebel if you know how to rule in a spirit of moderation and wisdom.

It is good to know not only how to make your servants obey but how to make them love and revere you. I find that the best way to make the impression of a real master is to do what I told my wife to do, talk as little as possible with her maid and even less with other servants. Too much familiarity kills respect. I also told her to give her orders in detail and at frequent intervals. She should not act like some people, who call everyone together and announce, "one of you do this," and then, when no one does it, all are equally at fault and no one is personally responsible.

I also said that she should order maids and all her servants never to leave the house without permission. They should all be on call and ready to help. She was never to give permission to all to go out at once, for there should be someone in the house on guard at any time. If anything happened, someone should always be there. I have always preferred to organize my house so that at any hour of the day or night, one person in the house was in charge in case something came up. There should also always be geese and dogs in a house, animals that are watchful and, as you know, both suspicious and affectionate. One wakes the other and calls out the whole crowd, and so the household is always safe—that is my way. To return to our subject, however, I told my wife not only never to give them all leave to go out at the same time, but also, if they came in late, to insist firmly, gently, and with deliberation on knowing the reason for it.

Besides this I said: "Since it does often happen that among servants, however obedient and reverent, occasional disagreements and conflicts arise, I charge you, dear wife, never to interfere in any such quarrel. Don't ever give any member of your household cause to feel that, in act or word, he can overstep what ought to be his bounds. Don't listen, dear wife, or show favor when one of them reports evil of another or brings an argument to you. The household full of quarrels can never abide in constancy of plan and purpose and, therefore, can never serve you well. If someone thinks that he has been injured through another's report to you and through your listening to it, he will carry a fire in his bosom and always be watching for a chance to revenge himself. In many ways he will try to make you condemn that person. He will be delighted to find that the other has committed some grave offense against the service of our house, for which he may be sent away. Should this wish of his be fulfilled, he will also feel free to contrive a similar disgrace for anyone else he dislikes. But if anyone can at his whim cause someone else to be discharged from our household, don't you see, dear wife, that he is no longer our servant, but our master? Even if he cannot quite gain his ends, he can keep our household in a state of agitation. He will be constantly thinking how, since he may have lost your good will, he can manage best for himself. He does not care at all if his profit be our loss. Even after he has left your service, such a man will keep trying to lay the blame on us and thus excuse his own past conduct. As you see, there is danger in a servant who speaks ill of the other servants and quarrels with them, whether you keep him or send him away. In either case he brings public disgrace. If you keep him, besides, you must always be changing your household staff, for people who don't want to serve our servant will always seek new masters. For this they will excuse themselves and cast the blame on you. Their words will get you a reputation for being either proud and aloof or avaricious and petty."

The truth is, my children, that when there are quarrels in the household, the masters inevitably suffer part of the harm done. But if the masters are not unwise, the house will not be quarrelsome. It is the poor judgment of the master that makes some families shameless and undisciplined and, as a result, always turbulent, poorly served, loaded with practical difficulties and public ignominy. The father of a family must detest talebearers, who are the source and cause of every quarrel, conflict, and intrigue. He should discharge them instantly. To see his household free of argument, peaceful, and harmonious should make him happy. This excellent state is one he can make sure of if he so desires. He must only do as I instructed my wife—never lend his ear or his mind to any sort of complaints or quarrels.

I further said to my wife that if a member of the household failed to obey her or to be as amenable and devoted as the peace and quiet of the family required, she should never be provoked into fighting with him or screaming at him. "It is an ugly thing," I said, "if women like you, dear wife, who are honorable and worthy of all respect, are seen with wild-eyed contorted expressions, screaming, threatening, and throwing their arms about. All the neighbors would reprove and mock you, and you would give everyone something to talk about. A woman of authority, such as I hope you, dear wife, will gradually come to be, maintains a constant modesty and dignity of manner. She would be grievously mistaken, not only if she raised her voice in reprimanding members of the household but if in commanding and discussing things she used a very loud voice. Some women talk in the house as if the whole family were deaf, or as if they wanted the whole neighborhood to hear every word. This is a sign of arrogance, a peasant habit. It suits the mountain girls who are used to calling to each other from slope to slope. You, dear wife, should admonish people with gentleness of gesture and of words, not with an air of indulgence and laxness but with calm and temperance. You must give orders in so reasonable and moderate a way that you will not only be obeyed but, because you show kindness and all the modesty compatible with your dignity, obeyed with love and devotion."

Lionardo: Where can you find such good advice for the edification of a perfect wife and mother as in these instructions of Giannozzo's? First he shows her the necessity of seeming and being most honorable and chaste; then he teaches her how to make herself duly obeyed, feared, loved, and respected. We ourselves shall be fortunate husbands if when we are married we have the wisdom to make use of your remarks, Giannozzo, and to teach our own wives to be like yours—shining examples of so many virtues!

But when you had showed her, as you say, how to maintain the modesty and discipline essential if she would rule the family, did you also show her how to preserve things and put them to good use?

Giannozzo: Indeed, on this point, what I shall tell you will make you laugh.

Lionardo: Why, Giannozzo?

Giannozzo: Dear Lionardo, my wife, being of the purest simplicity and free of any shade of cunning, thought that after listening attentively to me she was all ready to be a wise mother. I mentioned to her, then, that a good wife and mother must not only have the best of intentions, but must know how to carry out her tasks. I asked her if she had all the knowledge needed for this. Since she had always observed her mother's household functioning smoothly, she answered in all simplicity that she thought she was quite well instructed in these matters.

"Good, dear wife," said I, "I am glad to hear how competent you are. I do think it is your intention to make yourself in every way a perfect wife and mother. May God help your good will and preserve your fine character. Tell me, though, dear wife, how would you go about things generally?"

Lionardo: What did she say to that?

Giannozzo: She answered very eagerly, yet with a little blush of shyness in her cheeks. "I would do well, wouldn't I," she said, "to keep everything locked up properly?"

"No, indeed," said I. And you know, dear Lionardo, the illustration that then occurred to me I think will please you. Said I to her. "Dear wife, if you put into your marriage chest not only your silken gowns and gold and valuable jewelry, but also the flax to be spun and the little pot of oil, too, and finally the little chicks, and then locked the whole thing securely with your key, tell me would you think you had taken good care of everything because everything was locked up?"

At this she lowered her eyes to the ground and seemed silently to regret her haste in answering before. I was no little pleased inwardly, seeing that becoming air of repentence on her face. I could see that she was indeed aware of having been too quick to answer me and that she would, in time, become more and more careful of her words, more mature, more deliberate. After a little while, with humble and modest slowness, she lifted up her eyes to me and, without speaking, smiled.

Said I, "Do you think the neighbors' wives would admire you if, when they came to call on you at home, they found you had locked up the house to the very threshold? I'm sure you realize, too, dear wife, that to lock up the chicks with the flax would mean trouble, to put the oil in with the clothes would be risky, and to lock up things that are used every day in the house would be small wisdom. It is best, therefore, not, as you say, to lock everything up properly, but to be sure everything is in its place as it should be, and not just in its place, but so arranged as to do no harm to something else. Everything should be set where it is absolutely safe, yet accessible and ready to hand, while encumbering the house as little as possible.

"You have now seen, dear wife, where everything belongs. If you think something would be better placed elsewhere, more convenient and more securely locked, think it over carefully and then arrange things better. And so that nothing gets lost, just be sure that when something has been used it is immediately put back in its place, where it can be found again. If something has been mislaid or lent to a friend, you'll be able to see that its place is empty. You can set about getting it back at once, so that nothing will be lost through negligence. When you receive it back again, you must put it back in its place. If it should be locked up, lock it up and be sure the key is in your keeping, for you, my wife, will have to keep in your custody and to preserve whatever is in the house.

"To do this well, however, you must not spend all day sitting idly with your elbows on the window sill, like some lazy wives who always hold their sewing in their hands for an excuse, but their sewing never gets done. You, instead, should take up the pleasant task of inspecting the house from top to bottom more than once a day. You should check whether things are in their places, and see how everyone is working. Praise the ones who perform their tasks the best, and if someone is doing something one way which could be done better in another, show him the better way. Altogether avoid idleness, always keep busy. Being busy will make you a better housekeeper and will help you greatly in every way. You will eat with a heartier appetite. You will be healthier, better complexioned, fresh and lovely. Your household, too, will be better run, and your people will not be able to let things go to waste."

Lionardo: You are certainly right. When the servants are not afraid they will be seen and no one watches them, they throw more away than they ever wear out.

Giannozzo: There are dangers beyond this, too. They become greedy and lascivious. From the master's neglect they take encouragement to indulge in idleness and in greater vices. I told my wife to be as diligent as she could be, making sure things were arranged reasonably and properly in the house. She must not, I told her, permit anything in the house to be used that was not needed. She must save the surplus of things, and keep it safe. If some object is of no use to the household, let her put it aside to sell, and always be more pleased to sell than to buy. With the money let her buy only what the family needed.

Lionardo: Did you teach her how to decide whether something was really superfluous?

Giannozzo: I did. I said to her, "Dear wife, anything without which we could honorably supply our needs is a luxury. It should not be left to lie about the house and get into everybody's hands, but should be put away. Our silverware which is not used every day you put in its place until the occasion arises of our entertaining honored guests; then you display it on the table. Likewise things used only in winter should not be left lying about in summer. What is only used in summer should be put away in winter. You should consider anything you are able to save without depriving the household as a luxury in this sense. You should save it, put it away, preserve it.

Lionardo: And didn't you give your wife a system for saving things?

Giannozzo: Yes, I did. "First," I said, "if you want to save things, you should see that they don't spoil just by lying around. Second, you should see that they are not eaten or destroyed by others. Therefore, it is necessary to put things away where they will keep well—grain in a cool place, open to the north, wine in a spot that is neither too warm nor too cold and where no draft or bad odor can damage it. Things must be watched so that if part has begun to spoil, it can be immediately made good or used before it becomes altogether useless or treated so that it will not deteriorate all together. It is also essential to store such things well away in a place where everyone cannot use or destroy them." This I told her, and in this case, I said, I would not blame her for using lock and key to keep things from falling into the hands of the whole company. I would insist, too, that those keys should remain always in the custody of the mistress of the house, who would see that not too many hands touched them but that they stayed with her. Only keys used every day, like the pantry keys and those to the storeroom, should she put into the keeping of one of the best servants, the most loyal and honest, the most trained and scrupulous and conscientious about our property.

Lionardo: And would you give those keys to whoever had to go up and down getting things as they were needed?

Giannozzo: I would, if only because it would be annoying for the lady of the house to be forever handing out the keys and demanding them back. But I also said, "Dear wife, see that the keys are always in the house. When they are needed, we do not want delays looking for them.

"Also see that the man you put in charge of the other servants gives all of them enough so that they are spared hunger and thirst. If they lack necessities, they will serve us poorly and not give zealous care to our concerns. To healthy servants you will see that good things are given, so that none of them grows ill; for those who are not healthy you must arrange a proper diet and take good care to restore them to health. It is mere thrift to cure them quickly, for while they lie ill you can get no service from them and all you have is the cost of maintenance. When they are healthy and free, they will serve you all the more faithfully and devotedly. Thus, my dear wife, you should see that everyone in the house has what he needs."

Beyond this, I added another point. "Dear wife, be sure that the supplies you need for this and other household needs do not run short. Do just as I do with things outside the house. Think well ahead and consider what you are going to need, how much of each thing is already in the house, how much you usually need, how long the supply will last, and how much more is wanted for our use. Then you will easily know when the supplies need replenishing and will tell me at once, long before anything actually runs out. That way I can set to work to find it outside at the lowest cost and the highest quality. Things bought in haste are often bought out of season, unclean, about to spoil, and expensive. Then in the end more is thrown away than ever gets used."

Lionardo: And did your wife act to make provision and to keep you informed, as you taught her?

Giannozzo: Yes. As a result I have always had time to obtain the best of supplies.

Lionardo: Is it thrifty always to buy the best?

Giannozzo: Yes, indeed, it is the height of thrift. If you get wine that's too strong or rotten vegetables or anything else that is not good for the provision of the household, no one, I think, is going to be careful with it. The stuff is thrown out, spilled, no one cares, everyone dislikes it, and they serve you less well for this reason and consider it a sign of avarice, for which they call you mean. All you get is damage and disgrace, and people learn neither to love nor to respect you, since they dislike your miserable provisions. But if you have good wine, better bread, other things that are adequate, the household will be contented and happy to serve you. If the provisions are good, the steward is careful when he is doling them out, but with poor supplies he is as discontented as everyone else. Your household will cherish good things, and outsiders will honor you. Good things also always last longest.

Look at this gown I am wearing now. I have spent a good many years in it, for I had it made at the time of my first daughter's marriage, and I was honorably attired in it on all holiday occasions for a number of years. Now, as you see, it is still not too bad for everyday use. If I had not then chosen the best cloth in Florence, I might have had two for the price, but I would not have been as well dressed in them as I was in this one.

Lionardo: They do say good things cost less than shoddy ones.

Giannozzo: No doubt about it. The better things are, the longer they last, and they do you more honor, and make you happier, and are viewed by others with more respect. We want good things in our household, and an adequate supply of them. The saying "better scarce in the market than too much in the house," which some hold true, has always seemed to me adapted only to a poorly run family and one that lacks all discipline. If one knows how to rule oneself and one's family in an orderly way, one should have the house provided for in full and abundant supply. It would be hard to convey the degree of harm which mere disorder does or, on the other hand, to explain the real value of discipline. I don't know which is more damaging to families, the neglect of the father or the lack of discipline within the house.

Lionardo: Did you tell your wife how important it is to preserve this kind of order?

Giannozzo: I omitted nothing on that score. I found innumerable ways of praising good order and of casting disapproval on disorder of any kind.

To describe all that would take a long time. I showed her the necessity of good order, how things are happily and well done where there is good discipline. Finally, after many explanations, I gave her this parable to think about. "Well, dear wife," I said, "suppose it were a solemn holiday and you went out in public with your maids and servants walking in front of you. And suppose, as you walked very straight and elegant behind them, you wore a brocade gown, and had your head tied up for going to bed, and bore a sword at your belt, and carried a distaff in your hand. How do you think people would look at you? Do you think you would be generally respected?"

Lionardo: Notice the vivid image, Battista and Carlo. What an excellent figure of speech. But how did she reply, Giannozzo?

Giannozzo: "Surely," she said, "I'd be thought mad, poor me, if I dressed like that."

"Therefore, dear wife," said I, "we should have order and system in all that we do. It does not befit a woman like you to carry a sword, nor to do other manly things that men do. Nor is it always and in all places fitting for a woman to do everything that is proper to woman, for instance holding a distaff, wearing gold brocade, having one's head tied up in a kerchief. These things are all proper in their place and time. Your duty, dear lady, shall be to stand first in the household, not to be aloof and proud but with great gentleness to keep the whole house in order and in harmony through your conscientious supervision. You shall see that things are done in their proper time. What is needed in autumn is not to be consumed in May. What should be enough for a month is not to be used up in a day."

Lionardo: Did your wife seem amenable to your directions?

Giannozzo: She stood quite lost in thought for some time. Then I said to her, "My dear wife, these things I have been telling you will all, if you are well disposed to do them, prove easy for you. It should not seem hard to you to do what will win you praise. Rather it should weigh heavy on you to omit anything which you will be blamed for omitting.

"Up to this point I think you have understood all that I have said without any trouble and I am well pleased. As it was easy for you to follow these lessons, it will also be pleasant for you, I assure you, to put them into practice. Loving me and wishing to do the best for us both, you will put your mind to doing a good and orderly job of applying my teaching. And, dear wife, if you do something willingly, though it be difficult, you will do it well. Always when we are doing something we don't really want to do, though it be easy, we do it less than well.

"I don't want you to do everything, however. There are many tasks which you should not properly take on yourself. There are others to do them. Even in minor matters, however, it is up to you to give the orders. You must always, I tell you again and again, always be aware what everyone is doing."

Lionardo: What a fine and most pious lesson you gave your wife: to wish to be as well as to appear a woman of honor, to command the household and to make herself respected, to care for the welfare of the family and to preserve the things that are in the house. How proud she must have been to be the wife of such a man!

Giannozzo: You may be sure she knew I was telling her the truth. She knew I was speaking out of concern for her own well-being, and she knew too that I was wiser than she. She did, therefore, always have the greatest love and reverence for me.

Lionardo: What a great help, what a wonderful thing, to be able to teach one's family! Do you think she felt much gratitude for this, too?

Giannozzo: The deepest gratitude. She often used to say, in fact, that all her wealth and fortune lay in me. To other women she always said that I was her one adornment. I used to say, "Dear wife, your real adornment and your real beauty are found in your modesty and virtue. Your wealth is rooted in your diligence. For diligence is a more praiseworthy quality in a woman than beauty. Your beauty never made the house prosperous, but by our diligence it grows rich indeed. Thus, my dear wife, even more than beautiful, you should be and appear diligent, modest, and discreet. Thus let all your good fortune depend only on yourself."

Lionardo: These words must have kindled such feelings in her heart that all her thoughts and her whole mind never ceased striving to please you in every way. She must have sought constantly and labored strenuously to do everything right, never resting from her diligent care for the household, in order to show you that her zeal and love were all they should be.

Giannozzo: In fact she was at first somewhat timid about giving orders, for she had been used to obeying her mother. I also saw her inclined to remain inactive and to be somewhat melancholy of mood.

Lionardo: Did you do anything to remedy this?

Giannozzo: Oh, I remedied it. When I came home I always greeted her with a cheerful face, so that, seeing me happy, she too grew happier. She found no cause in my sadness to become sad herself. I also told her about a friend of mine, a very wise man, who used to know at once when he came home whether his wife, a rather difficult woman, had quarreled with anyone, for if she had she was sure to be less happy than usual. In this connection I voiced my hearty disapproval of all contention in a house. I also said that wives should always be contented in their household, both in order not to seem bizarre, like the bitter and quarrelsome ones, and in order to delight their husbands. A happy wife will always be more beautiful than a frowning one. "Remember, dear wife," I said, "that when I sometimes come home in a rather sour mood, as happens to us men after we've spent the day talking and contending with malevolent, scheming persons and with enemies, it always makes you sad as well, and really unhappy. So you must imagine it is the same with me, only more so, since I know your spirits can only be drooping through the unfortunate results of your own mistakes. You need do nothing but live happily, make sure the household obeys you, and keep the family well. I am doubly grieved when I see you sad, for I know that by your very unhappiness you are confessing some fault."

I repeated this notion and similar ideas to her several times. I encouraged her wholly to avoid melancholy of any kind. She should show a face of guiltless joy, affection, and affability to my kinsmen and friends.

Lionardo: I am sure she had no trouble recognizing her kinsmen, but I wonder if such a young girl would easily know who was a friend. We find that there is really nothing more difficult in the world than to distinguish true friends amid the obscurity of so many lies, the darkness of people's motives, and the shadowy errors and vices that lie about us on all sides. I should be glad to learn, therefore, how you taught your wife to distinguish a friend from a foe.

Giannozzo: No, I did not try to teach her to distinguish my true friends. This kind of knowledge, as you say, is all too fallible. We can hardly tell who is our true friend in spirit. But I did teach her to know for certain which were our enemies and whom she might consider as friends. "Never, dear wife," I told her, "think of someone as our friend if you see his energies directed against our benefit. If anyone wants to reduce our honorable condition in any way, count him for an enemy. For dignity ought to mean more than property, and honor more that comfort. The man who steals some of our possessions injures us less than the one who brings us disgrace. Now, there are only two ways of dealing with enemies, my dear. One is to defeat them in open fight; the other is flight, if one is weak. Men ought if possible to fight and win, but women have no alternative but flight for their safety. Flee, therefore, and do not let your eye rest on any enemy of ours. Call only him a friend whom I honor when he is present and praise when he is absent."

Thus did I speak to her, and thus did she act thereafter. She was most chaste and most content. She ruled the family wisely and took good care of the household. Her only failing was that sometimes, showing a mistaken zeal, she tried to do things that were below her. I, however, would instantly forbid this and tell her to let others do it. I insisted that she make herself the object of firm respect among her domestics by always behaving as the lady and mistress of all. Outside the house, too, she had to maintain a certain dignity. On a few occasions, in order to teach her a certain air of authority and to have her appear as she should in public, I made her open our own door and go outside practicing self-restraint and grave demeanor. This led our neighbors to observe her air of discretion and to praise her, which increased the respect of our own servants.

Lionardo: It seems only reasonable to me that the lady of the house should command respect.

Giannozzo: It has always been not merely reasonable but essential. If the lady of the house cannot command proper reverence and respect, the household does not obey her. Everyone does what he likes, and the family lives in turmoil and squalor. If the wife is vigorous and discreet, however, in carrying out her tasks, everyone will obey her. If her conduct is exemplary, all her house will revere her.

At this point in our conversation, Adovardo came among us. Giannozzo and Lionardo rose to meet him. Carlo and I immediately went upstairs to see if we could do anything for our father or if we might visit him. We found servants standing at the door to his room, with orders to let no one in. We were amazed and came down again to hear Adovardo explaining to Giannozzo that Ricciardo had spent the whole morning going over secret records and documents and that he was now alone with Lorenzo, who appeared to be doing much better.

Had I realized Ricciardo would be so busy today, *Giannozzo replied,* I would not have stayed on here like this, but would have gone in the middle of the morning to praise God and to adore the sacrifice, as I have done every morning for many years.

Adovardo: An excellent habit. A man who would emulate you in winning the love and favor of his fellow men should always seek first the favor of God.

Giannozzo: To me it seems proper also to render thanks to God for the gifts which he in his mercy has given me. I also pray for tranquillity and enlightenment of heart and mind, as well as for our long continued enjoyment of health, life, prosperity, a fine family, an honorable estate, and good name and renown.

Adovardo: Are these the prayers you address to God?

Giannozzo: They are. Thus do I usually pray, every morning. This morning, however, they have kept me here. The time flew so as we talked that we did not notice how it went.

Lionardo: Remember, Giannozzo, that this was an act of parental piety which you performed here, and no less pleasing to God than your presence at the sacrifice would be. What you have been teaching us also is good and is sacred.

Adovardo: What have you been talking about?

Lionardo: The noblest of subjects, Adovardo, and at the same time the most practical. How delighted you would have been, too, to hear his many and most excellent ideas.

Adovardo: I know that where you are only the most worthy topics are discussed. I know too that all the ideas of Giannozzo are well worth listening to.

Lionardo: Giannozzo is worth listening to on all subjects, but on this one you would have found his remarks particularly interesting and wonderful. Concerning the management of the household, his remarks were elegant, wise, rich, and original.

Adovardo: Would I had been there!

Lionardo: You would have found it profitable. You would have learned that thrift consists no less in making good use of things than in being careful not to waste them, and how important it is to be most thrifty with those things which truly belong to us. You would have heard how possessions, family, honor, and friendship are not altogether our belongings, and how we ought to apply prudence in their management. This, you would have said to yourself, is a lucky day in my life.

Adovardo: I am sorry I was otherwise occupied. For truly, Giannozzo, nothing would have given me more pleasure than to have sat beside this disciple of yours here and learned something which directly concerns me today, namely the prudent management of the household. It seems to me, as we become fathers, we ought to grow in our wise management of things as our family grows in numbers.

Giannozzo: Don't be too easily persuaded, Adovardo, of what is not even true. Lionardo here has always been partial to me, and perhaps I gave him pleasure in talking about the household because he, who has no real experience of these things as yet, found it a novel subject. Now if I delighted him more in our talk than my words themselves deserved or than I even tried to do, you must give the credit not to me but to Lionardo's affection for me, which makes all my words seem golden.

How can I, by my words, win the approbation of educated persons like yourselves, who read and converse every day with divine intellects? You transcribe noble thoughts and fine, wise sayings among those ancient writers of yours such as are altogether beyond my scope. Certainly I tried to say something worth saying, but I lacked the knowledge and the skill to adorn my thoughts with eloquence, to organize well, to weave in examples and cite authorities and use fine words; for, as you know, I am ignorant of Latin.* What I might say on some other subject, with which I have less direct familiarity would be unworthy of attention, nor could I speak even of the management of the household on any basis but my long years of experience and the useful lessons they have taught me. So Adovardo, my dear, don't worry about what you have been missing. You have a wife and children; you experience and learn from day to day just what I have learned myself. As you are both more intelligent and more educated than I, moreover, you can comprehend more quickly and more deeply than I could what are the demands, the method, the system and all that belongs to good management.

Adovardo: Lionardo thinks no better of you than you deserve, and you, in discussing the subject of the household, could not help being most helpful. I would have been glad to listen to you, both for other reasons and in order to find out whether your judgment confirms my own opinions.

Giannozzo: Could I attain to a judgment on anything that was not entirely obvious and commonplace? On what question, Adovardo, would my opinion not be entirely outweighed by your thought and your education? I have always been satisfied to learn no more than I needed to know; it suffices me to understand the things I see and feel in my hands. You educated people want to know what happened a hundred years ago

---

* Literally, "illiterate."

and what will happen sixty years from now. On every subject you demand intelligence, skill, knowledge, and eloquence to equal your own. Who could satisfy you? Certainly I can't. I am not one of these people. And to tell you the truth, perhaps I am happier, Adovardo, that you were not present. Not that I respect the judgment of Lionardo less than your own, but I would then have had two of you educated folk to please— which might have disconcerted me into trying to seem what I am not. Then I might have said something foolish, and I would have been very ashamed realizing that I could not please you.

Lionardo: Rest assured, Giannozzo, as long as you were talking about the management of the family, educated people who were not peevish souls would gladly listen. I cannot imagine anyone wanting you to have a different style or material or manner of arranging your ideas.

Adovardo: I certainly would not have wanted you to deal with different material, and to tell the truth, Lionardo, I never would have believed that the subject of household management had so many divisions as you tell me Giannozzo found to distinguish.

Lionardo: And I didn't tell you half of it.

Adovardo: What?

Lionardo: There were many more points: that a family should have a house, a farm, and a place of business, so that they can all gather together and feed and clothe their children, and how one may take care of all these needs most thriftily.

Adovardo: And what about money? Did you say how one should manage money?

Giannozzo: Why speak of that? Is it not like everything else? Things must be used to supply the necessities, the surplus must be put aside in case of need, and help should be given to one's friends, kinsmen, and country.

Adovardo: You see, Giannozzo, here is a difference from what I myself had thought, and perhaps I did not arrive at my opinion without a good reason. It was my belief that a man need only know how to exercise proper thrift in regard to money in order to be an excellent householder. I came to this conclusion seeing how money appears to be the root of all things, or the hook to get them with, or the nourishment of them. Money, as no one denies, is the sinews of any kind of work. If a man has plenty of it he can easily fill all needs and satisfy a great many desires. With money you can have both house and farm and all the labor of men. All the crafts work like slaves for anyone with money. A man who lacks money wants for almost everything. One needs it for all things: the farm, the house, the workshop, all require servants, workers, tools, cattle, and so forth. And all these things are not owned or obtained without the expenditure of money. If money supplies our needs, however, why trouble our minds with the management of other things?

Consider, furthermore, Giannozzo, in these days of bitter misfortune and unjust exile for our family, consider how much less suffering has afflicted those of the Albertis who possessed money rather than lands. Consider how much less our family possesses now that they are here, because it was always their way to spend so much on buildings and land. Judge for yourself how much greater our property would be if we had been able to walk off carrying our houses and fields as we could our money. Do you doubt in the slightest that we would be better off if the value of those great properties there were paid to us here in cash?

Giannozzo: You educated people, as I have noticed before, are argumentative to a fault. There is nothing so certain, obvious, and clear but you with your arguments plunge it into doubt, uncertainty, and obscurity. Now, whether you are trying to debate with me according to the custom of such people or are merely interested in seeing what I think, I know it is my duty to give you a satisfactory answer, Adovardo, and not just to talk to uphold my position. I do not want to deny, Adovardo, that money is of some value as a means to supply our needs and satisfy our desires. I shall not admit on account of this, however, that you are right. Even if I had cash, many, many things would still be essentials which are either not always available on the market or not of good quality or too expensive. Even if goods were being sold cheap, I would still much prefer to perform the pleasant task of watching over my own estates, to plan for my own needs, to keep in mind whatever should be required, rather than spend my energy searching for things from day to day and give much more for them than if I had them coming in season to the house. If it were not for our time of misfortune, which makes you wish rather to have money here than land elsewhere, I think you would agree with me. If you had enough of an estate to fill your needs and wishes and those of your family, you would not be much interested in money. For myself, I have never seen the use of money if not to serve our needs and wishes.

If you really think money more precious than land, I must oppose your argument. Do you imagine, merely because you know that you yourself have lost less money than lands, that money is generally easier to preserve than more stable things? Do you imagine that the fruit of money is more useful than that of land? What is there that's more likely to go astray, more troublesome to get back, more easily dissipated, spent, and consumed in smoke? What is there more likely to disappear in all sorts of ways than money? There is nothing less stable, less solid. It is incredible what a lot of work it takes to hold on to money, and this is a kind of work more fraught with suspicion of other people, likelihood of trouble, risk of accident, than any other. There is no way to safeguard money, for if you keep it under lock and key, well hidden, then it does not serve you or your family. Nothing can be said to be useful if you cannot actually use it.

I could tell you more of the great perils money is exposed to: poor handling, deceit, poor advice, poor luck. Innumerable other catastrophes can swallow up all sorts of money at one gulp. Every bit goes down, and you will never even see ruins or ashes. Do you think I am mistaken about this, Lionardo, and you, Adovardo?

Lionardo: As for me, I agree with you.

Adovardo: Who did you say, Giannozzo, was so good at arguing that they turn every sure truth around with words? We educated persons? I would not want to deny my love of books, myself, but if educated persons are the ones who, as you say, can turn everything around and prove its opposite, then I must surely be considered an illiterate, so utterly do I now lack all means to confound your arguments. I shall not surrender too quickly, however, for you know, Giannozzo, there has always been more honor given to the man who wins against someone who defends himself than to one who defeats someone who gives up at once. Just for the sake of a more manly defeat, then, I shall assert that your argument does not entirely satisfy me. I cannot give any other reason but that it seems to me the movement and onslaught of fortune takes estates as well as money away, and perhaps sometimes money can be hidden somewhere, while lands and buildings stand open, exposed to war and enemies, and are destroyed entirely by fire and sword.

Giannozzo: I am glad to see you are like the wise old veteran fighters who use no less cunning than they do force, and who pretend to flee, sometimes, only to lead the enemy into some trap. Thus do you do, but you fortify your position with more cunning than strength. You shall be the judge of that, however. I will not be afraid of your snares, in any case, though perhaps I ought to be.

Consider, Adovardo, that neither the hands of thieves nor looting nor fire nor sword nor mortal treachery nor, I dare say, arrows, thunder, or

God's anger can rob you of your land. If the year brings heavy storms, floods, or much ice, if winds or heat and drought should rot or burn the seed, still another year will come to bring you better fortune, or if not to you, then to your children and grandchildren. How many wards, citizens of all kinds, have gained more returns from their lands than from money? You can find innumerable examples of this everywhere. And how many bankrupts, pirates, and such have used up the money of the Albertis? Inestimable wealth, enormous sums, riches such that one can hardly imagine them, have gone to enrich other men through our loss. Would to God these sums had been spent on meadows, woods, or some other anchorage which we might still call ours and which we might still hope to have back again in times of better fortune. Do not think money, therefore, more useful than estates; consider land precious and essential to the family. I don't know what use money was invented for if not to be spent and used in getting goods. If you have goods, however, what need have you of money? And goods have the further advantage, which money does not have, that they supply your needs.

Let us not entangle ourselves in this argument, however. Let us, like practical householders, leave debate aside. My conclusion is simply this: the good father knows all his wealth and does not like to see all in one place or all invested in one thing. If enemies attack or adverse fortune presses you on one side it is good to be strong and have resources on the other. If things are risky here, you save them there. If fortune does not smile on you in one enterprise, it will not strike you in the other too. I am not in favor, therefore, of having only lands or only money. Better have some of this and some of that, some stowed far away and located at a variety of places. The returns of all, moreover, should be used for your needs, and the surplus saved for the future.

Lionardo: Why do you look amazed, Adovardo, and almost dumb-struck by Giannozzo's words? Had you heard his earlier remarks, you would have seen that all he says of the management of the household is like a divine oracle. Every point was vital to the proper rule of the family inside and outside the house. Nothing was lacking, everything was uttered in a coherent way, all clear and lucid. You would have been full of praise.

Adovardo: If this be Lionardo's counsel, I shall willingly assent, Gian-nozzo, and I too shall judge that the good householder ought not to limit himself to money alone or to lands alone but should divide his fortune among various enterprises in various places. I shall be willing, then, to have him undergo toil and trouble in order to maintain and preserve things other than money, which is merely one thing among many. I had thought, however, that money was enough.

Lionardo: Would you think you could go wrong, Adovardo, in agreeing with Giannozzo's views on matters of good management?

Adovardo: No, indeed, it would be a grave error to think the judgment and the beliefs of Giannozzo imperfect. On some points, however, Lionardo, even if he is right, it seems to me no fault in a man to have some doubts. Good God, you have talked money down so much that, by your account, there is nothing lower—money merely serves as a means to buy goods. It seems to me you were trying to make money sound less valuable than it is. You put it in such a poor light, made it appear so much beset with dangers, that if men were ever to believe you, they would not even try to manage it with thrift. They might merely wish never to set eyes on it at all. Now though I see that in many ways you are right, yet I have a notion that money is a commodity which actually contains every other commodity. It seems to me you are forgetting here how, in one small purse, money enables you to carry about with you bread, wine, all victuals, clothes, horses, and every useful item. And who would deny the added usefulness of having money to lend to friends, as you say, and to do business with?

Giannozzo: Didn't I say you would be setting some snares for us, Adovardo? But the ways of you educated folk are too much for me. Nothing can be so carefully said but that you find fault with it. I lack the skill to strive with you in wit.

Adovardo: I certainly asked you what I did with no other purpose than to learn how you, in your wisdom, would answer this question. You have been dealing with questions related to it.

Lionardo: I shall answer, then, according to what I gathered from Giannozzo. I shall tell you how to deal with money. Every purchase and every sale should be transacted with simplicity, truth, good faith, and integrity. Whether you deal with stranger or with friend, all should be clean and straight.

Adovardo: Excellent. But what about lending money, Giannozzo? What if some noble lord asks you for a loan, as happens every day?

Giannozzo: I would sooner give him twenty as a gift than a hundred on loan. I would gladly avoid him altogether so as to have to do neither.

Adovardo: What do you think, Lionardo?

Lionardo: I feel the same way. I would rather lose twenty to gain a little favor than risk a hundred without assurance of getting any gratitude for it.

Giannozzo: Hush, don't say that—no one should ever hope for gratitude or favor from a noble lord. A great lord loves and esteems you just exactly as long as you are useful to him. He does not appreciate you for any good quality you may have, nor is it possible for a great lord to recognize goodness. Wicked, ostentatious flatterers and vicious gossips are always more common in the household of such lords than good men are. If you will stop and consider, you will realize that probably the majority of courtiers live in idleness and waste their time. They have no occupation by which to earn an honest living. They live on the bread of others and shun all work requiring industry and honorable effort. If there are good men among them, they live modestly and hope to get more favor by their virtues than by ostentation—these would rather be loved for their merits than for the harm they inflict on others. But virtue is not recognized unless it is put to some kind of work, and when that happens, and when it is recognized at all, the lord thinks it sufficient to give praise—rarely is virtue well rewarded.

If you are an honest man, you cannot hold converse with the scoundrels you find there, for they will take offense at your continence, your austerity, and your piety. Among wicked men you can find no use for your good powers. It cannot serve your honor to compete with wicked men for a prize: better let them win and seize the thing you wanted. If you persevere in such a contest, you will suffer more evil done you by those bold scoundrels than you will gain praise from other good men. Those bold and careless beings will overcome you. With one bad report the flatterers can do you more harm than much testimony in your favor can repair. I think, therefore, that a man should shun those great lords.

It is good to ask for and to receive things from them, believe me, but never to give nor lend to them. Whatever you give them is thrown away. They have plenty of people to give them things, both purchasers of their favor and persons who seek to repair some offense. If you offer them a trifle, you will be despised for it and lose the gift besides. If you offer them much, they will give you no payment for it. If you offer excessive bounty, still you will not satisfy their immense greed. They want enough not only for themselves but for all their kin besides. If you give to one, you create the necessity of satisfying all the others, and the more you give, the more trouble you draw down on your head. The more they hope for, the more they think they have a right to receive. The more you lend, the more you will have lost. With noble lords, your promises are obligations, your loans are gifts, and your gifts are thrown away. A man can consider himself fortunate if his acquaintance with great lords does not result in some grievous price to pay.

Messer Antonio Alberti had this to say on the subject: lords should be greeted with gilded words. You will find that noble lords who are in debt to you will grow displeased with you in order not to have to pay. They will quarrel with you and try to provoke some remark or some answer which they can use as an excuse to do you harm. They will constantly try most viciously to bring you to an unfortunate end. If there are many ways they can harm you, they will choose the worst.

Adovardo: Then I shall be prudent and, in accordance with your advice, shall avoid all dealings with great lords. Should I find myself nonetheless engaged in some commerce with them, I shall always ask for cash. If, in spite of all, a demand is made of me, I shall give a minimum.

Giannozzo: That is the way to act, my sons. By all means, avoid any sort of courtier's role and attendance on a tyrant. This will prove your best course.

Adovardo: And what of friends?

Giannozzo: Why ask? You know that with a friend one should always try to be generous.

Lionardo: Lend and give to them?

Giannozzo: You know well enough. Where there is no need, why should you give? Not to make them love you, for these are friends already. Not to show them your generosity, at least not when there is no need. No gift seems an act of generosity to me unless need calls for it. I am one of those who would rather have friends of noble character than rich ones, yet I am happier with friends who are prosperous than with unfortunate and poor ones.

Lionardo: But if my friend asks me for help, can I deny him anything?

Giannozzo: Don't you know the answer to that? You can deny him all that he asks that is not honorable.

Adovardo: But I think there is no dishonor in asking something from a friend when there is need.

Giannozzo: If to do what my friend asked were to impose too heavy a burden on me, why should I put his welfare before my own? I certainly want you to lend to your friend, when no excessive burden is put on you by it. Do it in such a way, however, that, when you want your own back, you will not have to sue him for it, and he will not become your enemy.

Lionardo: I don't know how much approval I shall win from you wise managers of these affairs, but I myself would give a lot of latitude to a friend in any situation, would trust him, lend to him, give to him: nothing should stand between him and me.

Giannozzo: And what if he did not do the same toward you?

Lionardo: If he were my friend he would. He would communicate all things, all wishes, all thoughts to me. All our wealth would be held in common, no more his than mine.

Giannozzo: Could you tell me of one you have found who gave you more than words and empty chatter? Show me one whom you can trust with even the least of your secrets. The world is full of deceit. Take it from me, the person who tries by some sort of art or cunning subterfuge to take from you what is yours, that person is no friend. He asks you for gifts or loans or he wants to gain these things by threats or come at them by flattery—I say he tries to steal from you and he is not your friend.

Adovardo: That is true. People who greet you, who praise and flatter you, are common enough, but not friends—as many acquaintances as you like, but very few persons you can trust. How, then, shall we act toward them?

Giannozzo: Do you know what a friend of mine does? In other ways his character is most upright and disciplined, but perhaps on matters of finance he is a little close. He has a technique for dealing with irresponsible people who come with their importunate demands under color of friendship, kinship, and old acquaintance. The greetings of such a fellow he returns with an infinite number of greetings. If he smiles, my friend returns a warmer smile. If he praises him, my friend praises him still more than he has been praised. The man is confronted by generosity in all these things, where he finds himself surpassed in liberality and kindness. To all his words and all his whining, my friend lends a willing ear, but when he comes to the story of his needs, my friend immediately invents some of his own to tell, and as the man comes to the point of actually asking him, in conclusion, for a loan or at least to stand surety for one—suddenly he is deaf. He misunderstands and gives a reply to something else, and quickly changes the subject. Those who are masters of the art of finagling, however, then respond to him with some little joke and, after that bid of laughter, return to the question. He then repeats his maneuver. When at last by continued persistence they make their request, if it is a small sum they are asking, he lends it to them to get rid of the nuisance and because he can find no excuse, but he lends as small an amount as he can. If the sum demanded seems large to him, my friend— but what a bad teacher I am! What am I doing? When I should be urging you to be courteous and liberal, I am showing you how to deceive and hold back more than you should. No more. I don't want you to call me a master of slyness. Toward friends one should have a liberal spirit.

Adovardo: No, Giannozzo, rather think it a virtue to overcome slyness with slyness.

Lionardo: Indeed, I often think some shrewdness is required in dealing with shrewd people.

Giannozzo: Then you would like me to give you a method of eluding such petitioners. If my teachings help you to fight artifice with artifice, I am well pleased. If instead they do you harm by helping you to be niggardly and narrow rather than liberal and generous, I am still pleased that at least you will have a way of seeming merely clever when what you really are is avaricious. If you take my advice, however, you will prefer the honor gained by seeming generous to the appearance of cleverness. Generosity combined with reason has always won praise, while cleverness is often censured. I do not admire good management so much, moreover, as to condemn occasional generosity, nor do I view generosity as the pre- rogative of friends alone—sometimes I think it is wise to show generosity toward strangers, whether to make it evident that you are not niggardly or to acquire new friends.

Adovardo: It seems to us, Giannozzo, that now you are employing your friend's technique with us, for in order not to tell us what we wish to hear, you have turned your discourse to another subject, namely liberality. We want to hear and learn about that friend of yours, so that we, too, may defend ourselves against petitioners such as annoy us every day.

Giannozzo: So you insist! I shall tell you, then. My friend used to tell these tricksters, first, that he did feel it was his duty to do all things for his friends, and yet that it was not now possible for him to do what he would like to or as much as was his custom and their right. Then, with an abundance of words, he would explain that it was not best for them nor necessary at the moment to spend that sum. He told them it was not useful to them, it was to their advantage to wait or to take some alternative course. He was thus generous and even prodigal with advice. Finally he would suggest to them that they ask someone else, and promise to do all he could to talk with friends of theirs about getting them money.

And if they continued to try to persuade him by repetitions of their request, he would finally say in exhaustion: "I shall think it over and find some good solution. Let's talk about it tomorrow." Then he would not be at home, or be too busy, and so the man would finally grow tired and prefer to look elsewhere.

Lionardo: But perhaps it would be best to say no in a forthright and manly way.

Giannozzo: At first that was my opinion, and I often used to reproach my friend. He would answer, however, that it was he who was right, for these devious fellows think they have found a way of petitioning us that we cannot deny. At the same time we must satisfy them without its costing us anything. "If I openly said no right away," my friend used to explain, "I would show that I was indifferent to them, and I would make myself an object of their hate. This way they feel they may be able to fool me, and I also show that I have some regard for them, and so, when in the end they see I have outdone them in shrewdness, they think the more of me. It is no small pleasure, either, thus to loosen the hold of men who hoped they had me."

Adovardo: I like this man well who, being asked for deeds, gives words —and instead of money advice.

Lionardo: But if someone of your own family asked you, as happens every day, how would you treat him?

Giannozzo: If I could do it without great loss to myself, and if it would help my kinsman, I would lend him all the money and property he wanted, all I could possibly lend. It is my duty to help my relatives with property, with sweat, with blood, with everything even to the sacrifice of my life, for the honor of my house and my kinsmen.

Adovardo: Oh, Giannozzo!

Lionardo: Noble, good, wise father. Thus should all good kinsmen be.

Giannozzo: Property and money are to be spent and made right use of. Those who don't know how to spend money except on food and clothes, who don't know how to benefit their kinsmen and the honor of their house, certainly do not know how to make good use of riches.

Adovardo: I must ask you another question now, Giannozzo. Pretty soon I shall see my boys beginning to grow up. Some fathers in Florence are accustomed to give their children a certain allowance for small expenses, and they believe the boys are less apt to go astray if they have a way of satisfying their youthful desires. They say it is keeping children on a tight leash with regard to money that drives them into many vices and wicked ways. What do you say to this, Giannozzo? Do you think one should be so openhanded?

Giannozzo: Tell me, Adovardo, if you saw one of your children playing with a sharp and dangerous thing, such as a well-sharpened razor, what would you do?

Adovardo: I would take the razor out of his hand. I would be afraid he might hurt himself.

Giannozzo: And you would be angry, I know you would, with whoever had let him have it. Right? But is it more proper to a child to handle razors or to deal with money? What do you think?

Adovardo: Neither one seems naturally his concern.

Giannozzo: And do you think a little boy can handle money without danger? Even I, at my advanced age, still find the use of money not without peril. That is the nature of money. Do you suppose it is not very dangerous to inexperienced youth? Let us leave aside the fact that greedy and insidious persons will take it all away from them, for young people find it very hard to defend themselves against such persons. What use do you suppose a young man has for money; what are the needs of a boy? His father feeds him at his own table. If he is wise he does not allow him to eat elsewhere. If the boy wants clothes, he can ask his father for them. His father, being kind and wise, will satisfy his desire, yet not permit him to dress in a licentious or frivolous manner. What needs or desires can a boy have unless it be to plunge into luxury, folly, and gluttony? I would rather urge fathers to teach their sons, my dear Adovardo, that they should not wallow in lascivious and dishonorable indulgence. If the boy does not wish to spend money, he does not need it. If your son's longings are honorable ones, he will be glad to inform you of them, and you will be kind and generous in gratifying him.

Lionardo: Yet, Giannozzo, prudent citizens do uphold this practice, and they would hardly do so if they did not see some good in it.

Giannozzo: If I thought that the will and the course of youth could be restrained at all, I would vehemently condemn the father who does not at least attempt to turn his sons away from their appetites before he decides to help them toward their satisfaction. The more I think about it, the less do I know which is more harmful to young people, needing money too badly or being too well supplied.

Lionardo: I gather that Giannozzo wants fathers first to try to turn the young people away from their appetites as much as possible. Then, however, I am sure, he does not want them made even worse by lack of money.

Giannozzo: Exactly.

Adovardo: Oh, Lionardo, Giannozzo is really helping me today.

Lionardo: He was an even more valuable teacher before when he set forth all that can be said of thrift, and how to manage property wisely, and how to rule the family. It seems to me Giannozzo in fact taught us how to apply thrift to all things, to everything one needs in life.

Adovardo: Don't you think, Giannozzo, that friendship, fame, and honor are useful in life?

Giannozzo: Most useful.

Adovardo: And did you teach the application of thrift to them?

Lionardo: That, no.

Adovardo: Perhaps you did not think that these were matters about which one could give instructions?

Giannozzo: On the contrary.

Adovardo: Then what do you say about them?

Giannozzo: For myself, what do I know about friendship? Perhaps I might say that a rich man will have more friends than he wants.

Adovardo: Yet I see the rich much envied by others. They say all the poor are the enemies of the rich, and perhaps what they say is true. Do you want to know why?

Giannozzo: I do. Go on.

Adovardo: Because every poor man wants to get rich.

Giannozzo: True.

Adovardo: The poor are almost innumerable.

Giannozzo: True, much more numerous than the rich.

Adovardo: And all of them struggle to increase their property, each with his art. They use deceit, fraud, and robbery no less than labor.

Giannozzo: True.

Adovardo: If riches, then, are surrounded by so many itchy fingers, can they be called a thing that brings friends or enemies?

Giannozzo: And still I am one of those who would prefer the self-sufficiency of wealth. I would be glad never to have to ask a friend for help. It will hurt me less to refuse those who ask for a loan than to lend to everyone.

Adovardo: Perhaps it is possible in time of peaceful prosperity to live without friends to sustain you. Don't you need them, however, to defend you against injustice and to assist you in adversity?

Giannozzo: I don't deny that friends are exceedingly useful in human life. But I am a man who asks for help as rarely as possible. Not unless an urgent necessity pressed me would I impose a burden on a friend.

Adovardo: If you had a bow, Giannozzo, don't you agree that you would string it and shoot an arrow or two in time of peace, to see how it would do in time of war?

Giannozzo: Yes.

Adovardo: And if you had a fine gown, wouldn't you want to try it on in the house sometimes, to see how it ennobled your appearance for feast days and public occasions?

Giannozzo: Yes.

Adovardo: And if you had a horse, wouldn't you want to make it run and jump to see how well it would bear you over difficult roads or carry you to safety?

Giannozzo: Yes, but what do you mean by all this?

Adovardo: I wish to point out that the same applies to friends. They, too, should be tested in easy and peaceful situations to see what they would do in time of trouble. In a private and minor way, they may show in a domestic situation what they would be worth in public and weighty affairs, how much they will do for your benefit and honor, how much they are likely to endure for you, to sacrifice for you in ill fortune, and in order to save you from trouble.

Giannozzo: I don't think these ideas of yours are without value. It is better to have tested friends than to be forced to rely on the hope that they will prove good. But to judge by my own experience, I have never injured anyone, always taken care of my own affairs, minded my own business, and gained by this a good many acquaintances. I do not need to ask for anything or to wear out my friends. I make my living honorably and do not, thank God, stand low among men. Let me encourage you, therefore, to go on as you do: live in honor and take no pleasure in doing anyone harm by word or deed. If you do not covet what belongs to others, if you know how to manage your own affairs wisely, you will but rarely have to test your friends, and then but little.

I would be glad to stay here with you as long as you like, but I see my friend for whom I must do something at the palazzo. It was arranged early this morning, and now it is almost time to go there. I don't want to forsake him. I always like helping others better than asking them for things. I would rather have others obligated to me than find myself under obligation to them. I like this work of piety, supporting and helping a man with deeds and words as best I can. I like it not so much because I know he is devoted to me as because I know he is a good and just man. Good men should all consider themselves friends. Even if you do not know them personally, you should always love and help good and virtuous men.

You will stay here, then, and we shall soon be together again. There is one thing I do not want you to forget. Keep this in mind, my children: let your expenses never exceed your income. If you can keep three horses, prefer to keep two that are nice, fat, and well groomed, not four that are hungry and poorly caparisoned. As you educated men say, the eye of the master fattens the steed. As I understand it, that means the household is nourished no less by your diligent care than by your expenditures. Isn't that how you would interpret this ancient saying?

Adovardo: It seems right.

Giannozzo: If you think so, then which of you, wise as you are, would not rather have two public witnesses doing credit to your diligence than four proclaiming your negligence to all the world? Right? Therefore do this: make your expenditures equal to your income or less.

Be in all things—in words, in thoughts, and in actions—just, truthful, and wise. Thus will you be fortunate and well loved and honored.

INDEX

This index pertains to the General Prologue, Prologue to Book III and Book III itself. It does not pertain to the Introduction.